WHAT
WOULD
JESUS
CRAFT?

_ _ _ _

WHAT
WOULD
JESUS
CRAFT?

30 Simple Projects for Making a Blessed Home

Ross MacDONALD

FLATIRON BOOKS
NEW YORK

Designed by Susan Walsh

www.flatironbooks.com

The Library of Congress Cataloging-in-Publication Data is available upon request.

ISBN 978-1-250-05942-0 (hardcover)
ISBN 978-1-250-05943-7 (e-book)

Flatiron books may be purchased for educational, business, or promotional use. For information on bulk purchases, please contact the Macmillan Corporate and Premium Sales Department at 1-800-221-7945, extension 5442, or write to specialmarkets@macmillan.com.

First Edition: November 2015

10 9 8 7 6 5 4 3 2 1

CONTENTS

INTRODUCTION

Crafting and Faith—A Marriage Made in Heaven

Like most normal people, you probably adorn your house, workplace, and vehicle with images of Our Glorious Savior. A cross over your bed, a plaque or two in the den and gun room, some praying hands on the TV, a couple of crucifixes dangling from your rearview mirror and neck—there is practically no surface in our lives that can't be beautified with some reminder of His ever watchful gaze. Of course you can purchase all kinds of store-bought faith-themed décor, but if you're a hands-on person like me, it's so much more uplifting to make them with your own hands! And—with the help of this book, those hands of yours, and a little imagination—you can craft things that no store would *ever* sell!

In this book you'll find beautiful crafts for your home, your pets, for Sunday school, things you can wear, and more. Some are easy, some are more challenging, but there are no complicated undertakings that require expensive or dangerous tools like arc welders, I promise! These crafts are designed with the simple in mind—if you've ever bedazzled a sweatshirt or made a yarn toilet paper cozy (and who hasn't?) then you are more than skilled enough for this book.

The Lord preserveth the simple.
—PSALM 116:6

In Crafting as in Life, Timing is Everything

As a young crafter, I was up for some crafting any time, anywhere. I was a wild man! You couldn't hold me down! But now I know that swinging a hot glue gun or a fistful of felting needles around the room while you're tired or half in the bag can lead to some scars and piercings—and not the interesting kind. And if you ever find yourself making hundreds of yarn pom-poms over and over, sitting at your kitchen table in your underwear, at the tail end of a three-day crafting spree, when your boss has been expecting you at the plant the whole time, you'll know you've finally gone off the crafting deep end. Just please don't ask me how I know these things.

So all I'm saying is, choose your crafting time wisely. Don't do it when you're tired or operating heavy machinery.

Waiting for the right time and place is something that Jesus could relate to. He bided his time before His first miracle, and it wasn't for lack of opportunities. Sure, He could have done six miracles before breakfast every day, but He didn't. No—he wanted to wait till the time was right. He saw plenty of sick and lame and blind to be healed all around Him—in those days the streets were probably clogged with them, and hordes of starving children besides—but still He waited. Our Lord and Savior was no show-off. Then one day the perfect opportunity came. He was at a friend's wedding party. And what a party it was (if you can believe the Bible, and I think you know we can). That party was swinging along just fine, and then the unthinkable threatened to bring things to a deadly halt—they had run out of (and at this point in the story you might want to brace yourself) *wine*! We all know the only thing worse than a drunken wedding reception is a dry one. It is a horror that cannot be borne. So Jesus knew He had to step in and do something. If there was ever a situation that called for busting out a miracle, it was now. That's how Jesus finally revealed His glory—turning six thirty-gallon pots of dirty foot-washing water into primo wine! I can't remember what happens next in the story, but I'm guessing the party was epic. And Jesus probably got a lot more invitations to parties.

For everything there is a season, and a time for every purpose under heaven.

—ECCLIESIASTES 3

The early bird gets the worm, but the second mouse gets the cheese.

—WILLIE NELSON

For Christ's and Safety's Sake

As my friend Lucky once told me, pointing his hook hand at his eye patch, better to learn from a bad example than to be one. There are tools and materials used in this book that you could seriously hurt yourself with, so play safe to stay safe. And if you know anyone who you think might be an accident-prone idiot, kindly steer them away from this book, especially if the idiot is also a lawyer.

Woe unto you, lawyers! For ye have taken away the key of knowledge. Ye entered not in yourselves, and them that were entering in, ye hindered.

—LUKE 11:52

TOOLS AND SUPPLIES

I won't attempt to list every single tool and material you'll need—see the lists at the beginning of each craft for that. But I did want to give a general overview. All the tools and materials used in this book can be easily found and mastered, and none are particularly expensive. I use a lot of things from tag sales and flea markets, and I repurpose household materials. The most expensive tool used in this book is the power drill, and if you don't already have one, you can buy a decent small cordless drill driver for under twenty dollars, or pick one up used for even less. All of the craft supplies used can be found at most craft stores.

Here are some notes on a few of the tools and supplies used:

1. HOT GLUE GUN. King of the crafter's tool kit. You can get one for a few bucks, but your best bet is either a dual-temp or high-temp glue gun. You can get a pro-quality one like the Surebonder HE-750 for around 20 bucks. While you're blowing your welfare check, why not buy a set of precision tips. More important is the glue itself. In most cases, you want a strong hold, and those clear glue sticks are just not strong enough. Get the yellowish high-strength sticks. You can buy them in the twelve-inch length, which makes life easier. The two downsides of the hot glue gun are burns and strings. The strings you learn to live with, but the burns can be annoying. One way to avoid most of them is to cover the tips of your thumbs and forefingers with a layer of flexible fabric first-aid tape. It won't get in your way, and it'll protect your fingers. If you prefer, you can substitute heavy-duty glue for the hot glue gun for most of the crafts in this book, but it will slow you down.

2. **GLUE.** **E-6000** is amazingly strong and dries fairly quickly. It is thick and hard to spread, so it's best for spot gluing. **Beacon Quick Grip** is amazing stuff—even stronger than E-6000, it spreads easier, and it dries almost as quickly as super glue. It is also paintable, unlike hot glue or E-6000. Fabric glue is indispensible for several of the crafts in this book. I like **Fabri-Tac** and **Beacon Gem-Tac**. They are both washable, very strong, and fast drying. Avoid water-based fabric glues. **Contact cement** is another glue that I use here. It is fantastic for certain uses—it is one of the strongest glues there is. If you are sensitive to fumes and chemicals, use it outside or in a very well-ventilated space. White glue or tacky glue is fine for many things, and it has the added advantage of being mostly odorless and nontoxic. The disadvantages are that in some cases it can be too gloppy or runny, and it's slow to dry and not strong enough for many applications. Super glue can be great for some things, but has limited applications. I rarely use it.

3. **KNIVES.** I use two kinds of knives in this book. The first is a **craft knife**. One brand is **X-Acto**. My main complaint with X-Acto knives is that the cutting edge is far longer than you need, which can make it dangerous to use. I prefer the **NT Cutter Art Knife**, which you can buy online. These knives are perfect for fine, intricate cuts but shouldn't be used to cut heavy materials; the blade is not strong enough. For that, use the **utility knife**. I like the **Olfa** version. It's strong, and because you only advance as much blade as you need, it's safer. The blade is strong enough to cut thin metal or tempered hardboard, and when it gets dull, you can snap off a section and keep going. For safety, wrap the snapped-off section in tape before you toss it. Although I didn't use one in this book, a rotary cutter is a good thing to have for making long cuts in fabric and paper.

4. **SCISSORS.** I have over two dozen pairs of scissors, each with specialized applications. Your crafting tool kit should have at least four. A long pair of good fabric shears for fabric only. A long general-purpose pair for making long cuts in paper, foam, or other materials (using a small scissors for long straight cuts leads to ragged uneven edges). A pair of strong utility shears—I like the **Olfa** serrated

edge ones—can be used to cut heavy materials like thick leather, card, and metal. Lastly, a pair of small precision scissors is a must for snipping the ends of threads, making intricate cuts, etc.

5. CUTTING RULER. You can get away with using only one cutting ruler, but since they are not expensive, make your life easier and get a few. I caution you against using those long, flexible, cork-backed stainless steel rulers for anything other than measuring or ruling pen or pencil lines, for which they work beautifully. They are terrible and dangerous for cutting. The cork backing means that the material near the edge of the ruler is not held down, and it can buckle and wrinkle as you cut. They are so thin and flexible that knife tips can ride up over the edge and onto your fingers. I've seen it happen repeatedly, and it wasn't pretty. I use a **12-inch Helix Safety Ruler** for most cutting. For longer cuts, a thick aluminum ruler is good. But **Non-Slip Quilter's Rulers** are a great thing to have in your arsenal—get a few. The 5 x 5-inch one is great for lots of small cuts, and the 24-inch will handle most long cuts.

6. DRILL. As mentioned previously, you can get a decent little battery-powered drill-driver for under twenty bucks. Look for one with variable speeds. Buy a set of drill bits, and you're set. You won't use it that often, but when you need one, you really need it.

7. HOLE PUNCH. For making perfect holes in materials, you can't beat a good hole punch. Those little office ones are only good for three sheets of paper—get yourself a serious hole punch. I use a revolving leather punch. It'll cut through almost anything, including quarter-inch steer hide and thin metal, and it has six different-sized tips. You don't need a fancy one—don't spend more than ten bucks.

8. PRINTER. In several places I mention using a waterproof inkjet printer. By that I mean waterproof ink. If your inkjet printer uses pigment-based ink, or if you have a laser printer, you're set. The **Epson Workforce** printers are good quality, fairly

cheap, and use a pigment-based ink, rather than the usual dye-based ink. It's totally waterproof when dry. If you have an inkjet printer with regular ink, don't despair. There are several products that you can spray on the surface of your prints so that they will be water resistant. Marshall's Image Guard is one, and Krylon makes several products. Spray them outdoors, and apply several light coats. Test them on your prints first.

9. GENERAL TOOLS. To complete your tool kit, you should have a couple of good awls, a pair of pliers, needle-nose pliers, a small saw, and a screwdriver. A ball-peen hammer and small bench anvil are great for setting rivets and other uses. Spring clamps are cheap and incredibly useful—get a few small and a few large.

Alright—enough blather. Let's get to work!

> Go to the ant, thou sluggard; consider her ways, and be wise.
>
> —PROVERBS 6:6-11

ART
MEETS
RAIMENT

Unto Adam also and to his wife
did the Lord God make coats of
skins, and clothed them.

—Genesis 3:21

LORD BOARDS (JESUS SANDALS)

A very wise man—it might have been Burl Ives—once said that to know a man you first must walk a mile in his shoes. Well, Jesus strode the rocky Holy Land in nothing but thin-soled leather "mandals," and after trying these out myself, I know one thing for sure—he had tougher soles than I do. After a short walk to the mailboxes I was about ready to hop up onto a crucifix, just to get off my feet. Try them for yourself. Every footstep you take will remind you of the pain He suffered for your sins.

You can make these with leather straps, like I did, or you can use leather laces.

MATERIALS
Piece of thick leather, about 8 x 12 inches. (8 to 10 ounce oak cowhide is best.)
2 pieces, roughly 8 x 12 inches, of thinner leather in a color of your choice.
   (3 to 4 ounce cowhide works great. Don't use deerskin; it stretches
   too much.)
Two 72-inch leather straps about ½ inch wide, or leather laces.
   (I used leather saddle strings.)
Contact cement and brush
Rapid rivets, small, #1 (If you use laces, you won't need rivets.)
Piece of heavy card, about 2 x 3 inches
4 small D-rings (optional)

TOOLS
Paper and pen for pattern-making
Utility knife, scissors
Leather hole punch
White pen or pencil
Hammer and anvil, or hard surface for setting rivets

INSTRUCTIONS

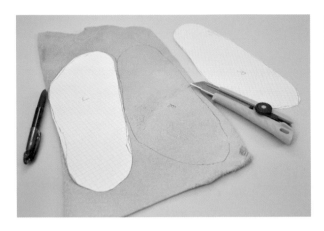

1 Stand on a sheet of paper and trace around your feet with a pen, leaving a little wiggle room around each foot—about a quarter inch. Mark the patterns L and R, respectively. Then cut out the pieces, place them on the thick leather, and trace around them. Mark the leather L and R also.

2 Cut out the pieces with the knife. Using those leather pieces as patterns, trace around them with the white pen or pencil onto the thinner leather. Cut those out and mark L and R on the suede side. These 4 pieces will be the soles of your Lord Boards.

3 Now cut 4 straps from the thinner leather, all about an inch and a half wide. Cut 2 pieces about 10 inches long and 2 pieces about 12 inches long (if you have small feet, you can use pieces that are an inch shorter; if you have large feet use pieces that are an inch longer). Place your feet on the soles, and mark where the straps should go.

4 Cut along your marks. Then brush some contact cement just inside the cuts, on the suede side. Brush about ¾ inches of the end with glue on one end of the shorter straps, on the suede side. Once the contact cement has thoroughly dried, push the end of the strap through one of the forward cuts, and stick the strap down onto the cement.

5 Time for a fitting! To begin, push the other, unglued end of that strap through its slit, then stand on the soles. Then push the straps in until they fit snugly around your feet, and mark where the strap enters the sole. Take off the sandals and transfer the mark you just made to the suede side of the strap, and brush cement on the end up to that mark. Once it has dried, push the strap through the slit up to the mark, and stick it down to the cement on the suede side of the sole piece.

6 The rear strap will be on an angle to fit properly, so push the ends through the slits, and do another fitting by placing your feet on the sandals, pulling the straps snug, and marking on the strap where they enter the sole.

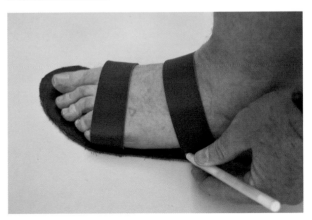

7 Again, transfer that mark to the suede side of the strap, apply cement and wait for it to dry. Then stick the ends in place. If you are using laces instead of straps, cut four 3-foot pieces. Push about an inch of the end through the front slits on each side and glue down beside the ends of the front strap.

8 Now glue your bottom soles down. Brush cement all over the suede side of the thick leather, and over the underside of the thin soles. When it has dried, carefully stick the pieces together. Remember, with contact cement you need to be sure that the pieces are in the right place before you put them together. Once together, you can't get them apart, so proceed with caution. If you are using straps for lacing, cut four 3-foot pieces. If your straps are thick, use the utility knife to slice off a layer of the suede side.

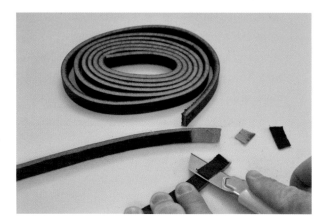

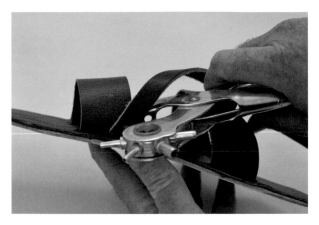

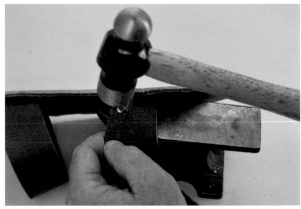

9 Position the end of the strap on the side of the front strap, down where it meets the sole, as shown, and punch it with the leather punch. Do the same for the other side.

10 Push a rapid rivet through, put on the cap, and tap it a couple of times with the hammer to set it.

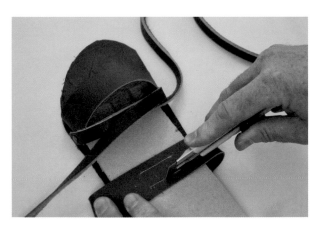

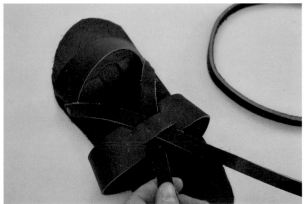

11 Mark where the straps cross the back strap, and cut 2 slits as shown, about an inch long. Put a piece of heavy card under the strap to avoid cutting the sole.

12 Push the ends of the straps through the slits and cross them. You can just tie your straps around your ankles, or you can rivet 2 D-rings to the end of one strap and use those to tighten the straps.

JESUS LOVES ME JEANS

It's a well-known fact that above all nations on Earth, America is favored by the Lord, and has been since its beginning when the first pilgrims set foot on it and claimed it in His name. Simply put, thanks to those Real Americans who uphold its values, America is the single greatest nation in all of human history. One of our greatest qualities is our generosity. Of the many, many bounties that America has graciously bestowed upon the world throughout our glorious history, blue jeans have got to top the list. They are simply the most beautiful, comfortable, versatile, and American pants going. And let's face it—the coolest. They are also the perfect canvas for personalization. Why not show the world where you're coming from, and let your hind end proudly shout that the Savior has got your blessed back!

MATERIALS

Small religious tapestry about 8 x 12 inches
Your favorite pair of jeans
Tracing paper
Fabric glue
Peel-and-stick fabric fuse

TOOLS

Scissors
Fine marker
Acrylic roller or metal spoon
Transfer paper (optional)
Thin leather, wood-burning tool (optional)

INSTRUCTIONS

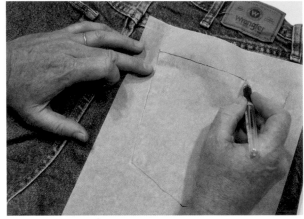

1 First you'll need a religious tapestry—try your local religious goods store or eBay.

2 Take your favorite pair of jeans and trace the outline of the outside edge of the back pocket onto tracing paper. The pockets should both be the same size, but double check by holding your pattern over the other pocket. If it's the same, proceed. If not, draw a second tracing paper pattern for the second pocket.

3 Cut out the pattern, place it on your tapestry, and try to find 2 perfect spots to cut out.

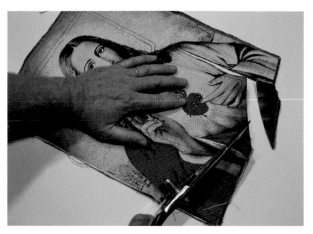

4 Now trace around the outside of the pattern with a fine marker and cut out the pieces.

5 Fold over roughly half an inch of the outside edge and glue it down with fabric glue. Make sure you fold over the same amount as the corresponding seams on the pocket. The side seams, for instance, are narrower at the bottom and wider at the top, so make your fold-over seams the same proportions. You can just eyeball these measurements if you feel lucky. If not, measure the pocket seams, and fold over your fabric seams the same amount.

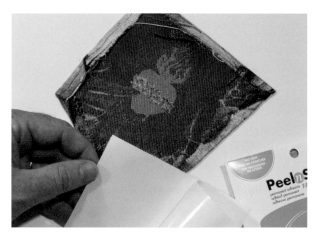

6 Put some peel-and-stick fabric fuse on the back. Use several pieces if you need to, and trim off the excess.

7 Now carefully position the fabric over the pockets on your jeans and rub down with an acrylic roller or the back of a spoon—and you're done!

8 But for extra credit, why not make a new leather tag, too! Trace the leather tag on the waistband for size. The new tag can be whatever you want. I went with "Jesus loves my ass." Now draw the lettering.

9 Transfer the lettering to a piece of thin leather using transfer paper.

10 You can use a marker to draw the lettering, but if you have one, a wood-burning tool is just the ticket! Plus, you haven't lived until you've huffed the aroma of burning goat hide.

11 Trim to size, and use more fabric fuse to attach your new label over the old one.

JESUS JEAN JACKET

No so-called "Canadian tuxedo" would be complete without the jacket. Update your old jean jacket by adding a back panel made from a wall-hanging tapestry rug. I rescued this beautiful tapestry from my Auntie Diamint's basement rec room. I felt bad for Jesus, staring at the decrepit Ping-Pong table for eternity. You can probably find one of these at a neighborhood yard sale. If not, then you live in the wrong neighborhood!

MATERIALS
Large tracing paper
Jean jacket or jean vest
Jesus tapestry, 18 x 24 inches (Try a yard sale or eBay.)

TOOLS
Marker
Scissors
Ruler
Hot glue gun
Needle and thread or fusible web (optional)

1 First, you'll need a pattern template. Place a large sheet of tracing paper over the back panel of the jacket and trace the shape with a marker. The back panel is the keystone-shaped piece of fabric in the center of the jacket's back. Add an extra half inch all the way around. Now cut the tracing paper along the outer marker lines.

2 Turn your rug over so the backside is facing you. You can see the design on the back of the rug, so use that to help you position your pattern. Use a ruler and marker to draw lines on the back of the rug, and then cut carefully along the lines.

3 The edges of the rug fray easily once it's cut, so fold over the extra half inch and hot glue it down.

4 Now you simply attach the rug panel to the back of the jacket. You can sew it down with a machine or hand stitch it, or you can attach it with fusible web and an iron. I couldn't wait to try on the jacket, and I already had the hot glue gun fired up, so I went for it, and hot glued the panel down. First I added a few lines of glue in the middle, then I ran a bead of glue around the outside edge, sticking the rug panel down as I went.

PRACTICE ANGEL WINGS

These realistic angel wings are suitable for cosplay or everyday wear. They're fun and easy to make, and you feel able to perform miracles when you wear them. Just don't attempt to fly—unless you want to really see some angels.

The first thing you need to know about making your wings is that feathers are either right or left, depending on which side of the bird they came from. And they come in all shapes and sizes; even feathers from the same bird. So to make realistic wings, you'll have to be selective about the feathers you use. I don't recommend buying craft-store feathers. They are small, poor quality, and expensive. You're better off buying from an online dealer like moonlightfeather.com. Or try eBay. You can get dozens of big turkey wing feathers for 12 or 13 bucks, and goose feathers are even cheaper.

MATERIALS
White turkey wing pointer feathers—about 8 left and 8 right
About 50 white goose feathers, 3 to 6 inches long
Wire coat hanger
Some thin brass wire, about a foot-long piece
2 pieces white felt
Package of marabou, or a white feather boa

TOOLS
Pencil
Hot glue gun, glue
Scissors
Pliers with wire cutter

INSTRUCTIONS

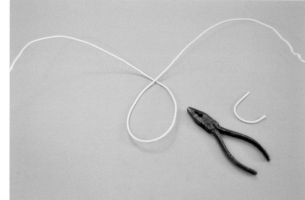

1 Sort your turkey and goose feathers into left and right. If you point the quills all the same way, you'll be able to tell the difference by which side is thinner, and which way they curve.

2 Untwist the coat hanger, snip off the hook using the wire-cutting jaws of the pliers, and bend into the shape shown.

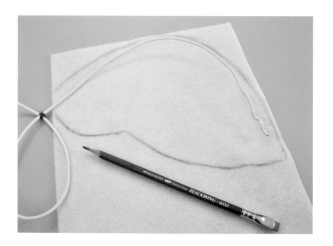

3 Make the wire loop about 4½ inches high and 2½ inches wide. Wrap thin brass wire around the part where the 2 sides cross. Now place the longer wire on one side on a 9 x 12-inch piece of felt, and trace the semicircular wing shape shown. As you can see in the photo, I've given myself lots of extra felt above and below the wire. The top of the curve, above the wire, should have about a half inch extra. That part will be folded down over the wire and glued to hold it in place.

4 Fold over the felt and glue down. I used the hot glue gun for this, but you can use any heavy-duty quick-drying glue. Choose your longest wing feather and glue it on the outside edge of your wing as shown. As you glue the next feathers down, overlap them and make each one a little shorter as you work your way in toward the center. Also note that we are looking at the underside of the right wing in this picture—notice how the feathers curve, and how the wider part of the feather is on the right. Make sure to orient all feathers on each wing the same way.

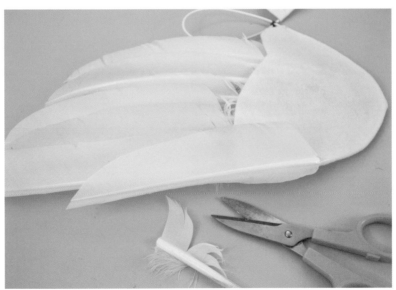

5 Glue down 7 wing feathers, and then turn the wing over. Trim and glue the 8th wing feather on the outside as shown.

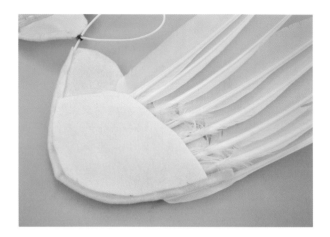

6 Turn the wing back again. Trim a piece of the leftover felt—about 9 x 6 inches—to fit as shown, and glue it down.

7 Glue your largest goose feather on the outside edge, and then work your way toward the center as before, overlapping the feathers. These feathers should rest about half on the felt and half covering the large turkey feathers.

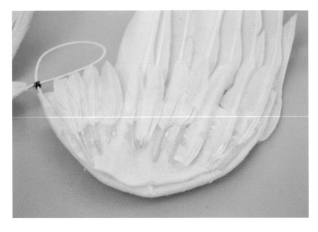

8 Now glue pieces of marabou over the quills of the last row of feathers. A little marabou goes a long way—you should only need about 4 to cover the quills. Then glue a final piece across the top of the curve.

9 When you complete the inside of the left wing, turn the wings over to work on the outsides. Glue down a row of larger goose feathers, just like you did on the inside, overlapping the large turkey feathers. You'll probably need a second row of the goose feathers here. Finish the top with a few pieces of marabou, and you're done! You can wear these by tucking the small wire loop down the back of the neck of your shirt or jacket.

FEDORA OF THORNS

Everyone who sees you sporting this jaunty chapeau will shout "Thank you!" for the graphic reminder of whom it was that suffered and died for their sins. Plus—admit it—it just looks badass.

MATERIALS

Medium grapevine wreath, about 9 inches across

Black or brown polymer clay

Tinfoil or parchment paper

Red crystal or stone beads

Fine brass wire

Gold paint

Your favorite hat—ball cap, visor, or fedora

TOOLS

Garden shears

Hot glue gun

Pliers

INSTRUCTIONS

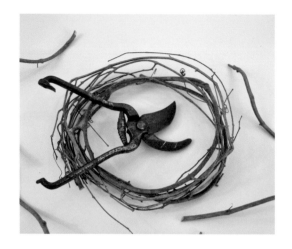

1 Unless you have a bunch of thorny vines lying around, use a medium grapevine wreath from the craft store or florist. We'll make our own thorns, and add "blood" beads. You'll need to trim the grapevine with garden clippers until you have 5 or 6 strands. The vines will already be woven and twisted together in the wreath, so cut away and remove extra vines, leaving the remaining vines twisted together. Trim the remaining vines until they are just long enough to fit around the crown of the hat, and overlap a bit at the back, about 24 inches.

2 Now for the thorns. You don't really want to scratch yourself baldheaded and bloody, so make the thorns out of something durable, but not hard. I used polymer clay. You'll need 25 thorns or so. Place them on tinfoil or baking parchment paper and bake for the recommended time and temp—usually around 275° for 10 minutes.

3 Now hot glue those bad boys onto your vine, spacing them out evenly. Glue them mostly pointing up and out, away from that beautiful brain and face of yours, for reasons that are hopefully obvious.

4 I had planned on using red crystal beads for the drops of blood, but these dyed stone beads looked perfect and the color really popped against the vines. Cut 2-inch pieces of thin brass wire and put one end through the bead hole and twist. Then twist the other end of the wire around the vines so the beads dangle below. Leave the wire a bit loose so the beads can move. For the final touch, paint the ends of the thorns so they look more lifelike.

5 Now mount the whole thing on your favorite hat and you are ready to make a public spectacle of yourself! The vines are very stiff, so your crown of thorns will stay put. If it tends to move, you can hold it in place with a stitch or two, or some glue.

PRAISE THE LORD T-SHIRTS

You have something to say to the world—what better place to do it than on the front of your T-shirt? Some people apparently want the world to know how rude they are, or what brand of beer they drink. But to us people of Faith, our shirt is a billboard to testify to that Faith. Every mega-church gift shoppe has racks of beautiful ones to choose from. But us crafters eschew store-bought goods we can craft for ourselves. Like many of you who've been into crafting for a while, I have drawers full of T-shirts decorated with homemade iron-on graphics, heat-set rhinestones, and puffy fabric paint. But this time, I wanted to up the ante a bit. Besides, most of my shirts seem to have suddenly shrunk a couple of sizes and I needed new ones.

Before you start, figure out what you want to say. I decided on a few shirts—"Jesus ROCKS!," "God made me," "Team JESUS," and my favorite, "Jesus loves me!"

MATERIALS

Tracing paper

Some T-shirts that fit

Piece of cardboard

Transfer paper in a color that contrasts your shirt color

Deco Foil adhesive, 2 ounce bottle

Deco Foil (The foil comes in several metallic colors, as well as pearl, leopard skin, and other patterns.)

TOOLS

Tape   Fine paintbrush

Pencil   Spoon

INSTRUCTIONS

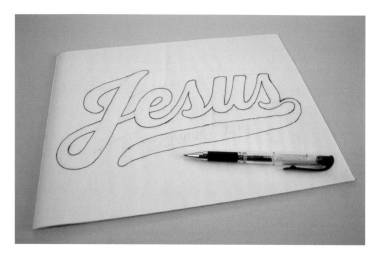

1 If you're good at hand-lettering, this first step should
be easy. If not, don't despair—just fool around on
your computer with your favorite graphics program
until you get something you like. Size it to fit on a
letter-sized sheet, print it, and then trace it onto
tracing paper.

2 If your shirts are new, wash them first. Then
put a piece of cardboard inside to keep them
flat, and to make sure the adhesive doesn't
soak through the fabric and get on the back.
Tape the transfer paper to the back of the
tracing paper, and then tape it to the front
of the shirt. Position the graphic about 5
to 6 inches down from the neck. Now use
a pencil to trace around your lettering, to
transfer it to the T-shirt.

30

3 The Deco Foil adhesive bottle has a fine tip that you can use to draw fine lines. For larger areas, squirt out a blob in the center, and use a brush to spread it. You want a nice nonlumpy coat of the adhesive if possible, but it's pretty forgiving. Let it sit for about a half hour to dry.

4 When the glue is dry, lay the foil on it and rub it down carefully, making sure to rub it all over the glued areas. Hold the foil down with one hand, and rub hard with the back of a spoon.

5 Now peel it up and marvel at your handiwork. If any areas have no foil, rub some down again. If it still doesn't stick, you probably didn't put enough glue there, but don't worry, you can add some and try again. After the shirt has dried for 12 hours, you can wear it. Follow the Deco Foil washing instructions.

BELT OF TRUTH, WITH SHIELD-OF-FAITH BUCKLE

We all remember making Armor of God costumes in Bible Summer Camp. Then you'd put on your construction paper Helmet of Salvation, Belt of Truth, and Shield of Faith, and whack the other campers with your Sword of the Spirit until the counselors made you quit. This version is more fun to make and a lot less lame, and the Belt of Truth now incorporates the Shield of Faith as a buckle! If the armor of God can shield the Faithful from the fiery arrows of the unbelievers, surely it can help you hold up your skinny jeans.

MATERIALS

Small piece of card, about 2 x 3 inches
Leather belt, at least an inch and a half wide
Rapid rivets, small #1 (from a leather
     supply store or online)
Leather punch
Charms and crucifixes
Thin brass wire
Large circular hook buckle
Parchment paper
Polymer clay, about 4 ounces
Empty tuna can
Adhesive foam letters
Gold gilders paste
Metallic bronze spray paint
Krylon Crystal Clear Satin spray fixative

TOOLS

Scissors
Pencil
White colored pencil
Wire nippers
Anvil
Hot glue gun
Sandpaper
Ruler
Small paintbrush

INSTRUCTIONS

1 First you'll need to make a lettering template. Cut a small piece of card the same width as your belt. Then line up 5 rapid rivets evenly across the belt, and mark their centers on the card as shown.

2 Lightly mark the letters on your belt with pencil (check to make sure they line up with the belt loops of your jeans or church slacks), and then using the template, mark the rivet positions using a white colored pencil. For the vertical lines of your letters, position the template on the belt so the top and bottom is lined up with the top and bottom of the belt, and the marked side of the template lines up with the vertical line of the letter. Then mark a white dot on the leather alongside every mark on the template. For horizontal lines, turn your template sideways, and line it up with the line of the letter, and mark the white dots again.

3 Punch out all the holes with the leather
punch. Now, doing one letter at a time, push
the head of the rivet into the hole, and then
turn the belt over, put the back piece of the
rivet in the holes, put the belt on the anvil,
and then tap each one smartly with the
hammer a couple of times to set them.

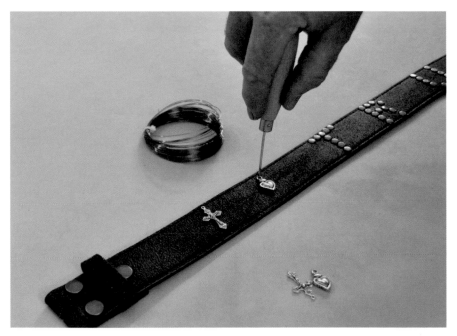

4 Position your charms on the sides of the belt that don't have letters
on them, and use the awl to punch 2 small holes in the belt—one
through the charm's loop, and the other about an eighth of an inch
above the first.

5 Snip a short piece of brass wire, and push it through the charm loop, and then through the holes. Twist it closed, trim the back, bend it flat, and tack it in place with hot glue. Also tack down the front of the charm to keep it from flopping around.

6 Now the shield buckle: On a piece of baking parchment, roll out 4 ounces of polymer clay with a bottle until you have a flat round slab about an eighth of an inch thick and 5 inches across. Then use the empty tuna can to cut out a disk.

7 Place the disk over the buckle, and gently massage it into a slight dome shape. Place in a 275° oven and bake for 15 minutes.

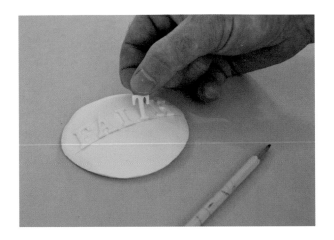

8 When it's cooled, sand it smooth, and then draw some lettering guidelines across the front with a ruler. Now place your foam letters. It's easier to space them evenly if you place the first and last letters, and then work in to the middle. Press the letters down firmly. You'll probably need to hot glue your shield to the buckle.

9 Spray on a coat or two of metallic bronze paint. When it's dry, brush gilders paste onto the front of the letters and around the shield, feathering it out to leave a dark background around the letters. Finally, spray on a coat or two of Krylon Crystal Clear Satin.

BE NOT AFRAID SAINT FRANCIS PET COLLAR

How could the Lord not *bless and protect any pet who sports this delightful collar, positively crusted* with Saint Francis charms? But just in case, it has the added protection of a beautiful crucifix tag. Your little Tippy will *jingle jangle jingle* as he goes striding merrily along!

MATERIALS

Leather collar

Leather punch

Some craft lace or other colored cord or thin ribbon

Jump rings (if needed for the charms)

Assortment of Saint Francis charms and crucifixes

TOOLS

Marker

Glue

INSTRUCTIONS

1 Use a marker to draw evenly spaced dots, about a half-inch apart, along the full length of the collar, and use a leather hole punch to punch holes. You can use an awl for this if you don't have a punch, but the punch makes cleaner holes.

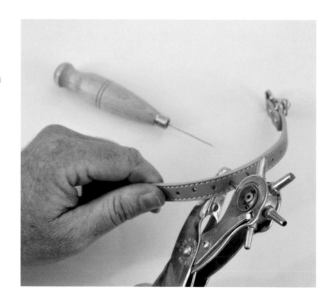

2 Using a contrasting or complementary colored craft lace, push the tip through the first hole in the collar from the back, lace it through the jump ring of the charm, and then back through the same hole on the collar. To make sure that your charms all face the right way when you're done, always hold the charm facing toward you, and push the lace through the ring in the same direction as you are lacing the collar—in this case, left to right. Don't pull the cord too tight—you want to leave a small loop so the charm hangs loosely.

3 Continue lacing, but leave the last 3 or 4 holes for the collar buckle. Then trim the ends of the lace and glue them down on the inside of the collar. Finally, attach the crucifix and whatever additional charms you want to the metal loop on the front of the collar. And now for the hardest part of this craft…Get the collar on your pet!

TOUCHED BY JESUS CHARM BRACELET

If, like me, you've always loved the look of charm bracelets and been fascinated by Catholic charms, then you'll go totally non compos mentis *over these saints, angels, and Jesus and Mary sparkling and cavorting on your wrist. Like most guys, if I wear a chain bracelet, I want it to be heavy enough to be used as a weapon in a Sharks versus Jets back alley rumble. So instead of the usual wimpy charm bracelet chain, I used a fat copper curb chain bracelet—beautiful and just strong enough to one day save your life.*

MATERIALS

Copper curb chain bracelet (drugstores carry them) or other heavy chain

Charms! (You can purchase all kinds of charms from Catholic stores, and lots of vintage charms on eBay.)

Medium-sized jump rings. I used brass because it looked good with the charms and the copper.

TOOLS

One or two pairs of needle-nose pliers

INSTRUCTIONS

1 Lay out your chain, and lay some charms along it until you get an arrangement you like.

2 Using the pliers, spread a jump ring apart and hook it onto your first charm, then hook it through the first link of the chain and close it again. The best way to open a jump ring is to spread it apart *sideways* rather than pulling the two sides farther apart (because the ring stays circular, and it's easier to close up again).

3 Make sure you close the jump rings tight or the charms may fall through the crack.

4 Work from one end of the bracelet and move along until you get to the other end. Put at least one charm on every link, and then check your progress—you may want to add more!

KEEP **THE FAITH** FLOPS

Where I live, wearing a shirt with buttons is considered "dressed up." Paired with clean flip-flops it's practically formal evening attire. It's enough to make one yearn for the days when my mother wore a hat and gloves to drive to the supermarket for a pack of Pall Malls, and even traveling salesmen and felons wore suits and ties. But comfort wins in the end I guess. So, for those modern formal occasions, why wear boring old plain flip-flops? With a little imagination you can gussy them up into something that just screams class and easy sophistication. You'll feel like you're walking on heavenly clouds in these, especially after you tried walking to church in your Lord Boards!

Now, it's a well-known crafting fact that no substance known to man will stick to plastic flip-flop straps—not contact cement, not the strongest hot glue, not even E-6000. And since you don't want to bust a move at a wedding reception dance and blind the blushing bride with a hurtling flip-flop charm, we'll be riveting some material to the straps, and applying our decoration to that. I'm using rapid rivets, but eyelets will also work.

MATERIALS

- 9 x 12-inch sheet of craft foam the same color as the flip-flops
- Pair of flip-flops
- Screw-on spikes
- Rapid rivets
- Deco Foil adhesive
- Deco Foil
- 2 baby Jesus figures from nativity scenes or king cake
- Charms

TOOLS

- Leather punch (or anvil, awl, or hammer)
- Paintbrush
- Hot glue gun

1 Measure and cut strips of craft foam to cover the straps of your flip-flops. Decide on the placement of the spikes. I placed 3 on each strip, about 1¼ inches apart, so there was room between them for a charm. Punch holes in the craft foam for the spikes and screw the spikes in place. Now place the foam strips on the flip-flop straps, punch a hole through both at one end, and fasten a rapid rivet in place. Then stretch out the strap and strip together, and punch and rivet the next hole. Work your way along the strap punching and setting one rivet at a time.

2 Now make your front ornament. Cut your 2 x 2-inch sunburst shapes out of craft foam and apply the Deco Foil adhesive to the top half of the shape. Once it has dried, press the foil onto it and peel off the backing.

3 Now glue a second quarter circle of craft foam onto the sunburst, and glue the baby Jesus to that.

4 Glue the baby Jesus sunburst down, hot glue the charms over the rivets, and take these bad boys out for a drive!

FOR YOUR BLESSED HOME

Through wisdom is a house builded; and by understanding it is established: And by knowledge shall the chambers be filled with all precious and pleasant riches.

—Proverbs 24:3-4

INFANT-OF-PRAGUE LUCKY LOTTERY TICKET CADDY

I read about a man in Connecticut who found his winning lottery ticket just over a year after the drawing. When he tried to collect, he was told he was too late. Oh you can bet he sued, but the poor fool's luck had run out. I was thinking about that loser, and my own pile of lottery tickets, and how I should craft somewhere safe to keep them, when I spotted the old bundt pan hanging on my Auntie's wall. That's how it is with us crafters—where others see old battered cookware, we see raw materials. And then it hit me—luck plus lottery tickets plus bundt pan equals the Infant of Prague!

The Infant of Prague is a surefire, time-tested, scientifically proven, miraculous money and luck magnet, whether you are a Catholic or a normal Christian. Put your lottery tickets in the bowl, place facing your front door, and get ready to answer when Lady Luck comes a knocking. And when she does, this lottery ticket caddy has a secret compartment for your winnings!

MATERIALS

Bundt pan, heavy aluminum if possible
Red and gold spray paint
Baby doll, roughly 6 inches tall
2 pieces red felt, 9 x 12 inches
Red and gold trim, roughly a yard of each
Small lace doily and 2 pieces of lace
   trim about 6 inches long
Spice bottle
Gold cardstock, a 5 x 5-inch piece,
   and a strip 6 x ½ inches
Small piece of polymer clay

Large blue marble
Pom-poms
Gold paint
Red and gold florist's marbles

TOOLS

Marker
Scissors
Hot glue gun
Craft knife

INSTRUCTIONS

1 Clean the bundt pan well with dish soap and dry. Spray the inside with 2 or 3 coats of gold metallic spray paint. When that's dry, set it face down and spray 2 or 3 coats of red spray paint on the outside.

2 Remove the doll's arms, and position it on the red felt and draw a quarter-circle shape as shown, 12 x 9 inches, and cut it out. Using that as a template cut the same shape out of the second piece of felt. Save a piece of the scrap felt for later.

3 Glue the gold trim along the bottom edge, and the red trim about an inch above that.

4 Glue the top edge of the back piece along the doll's neck like a cape.

5 Fold back the straight edges of the front piece. When you have the size and fit right, tack down the folds with a dot of hot glue, then glue the piece to the neck of the doll.

6 Cut out the center of the small doily and glue it around
the doll's neck. Then glue the lace pieces around the doll's
hands.

7 Put the arms into the gaps between the front
and back felt. You may need to cut a small
slit in the edge of the back felt. When you
get the position right, hot glue the arms to
the body of the doll. Tack the edges of the
front piece of felt to the back piece with a
couple of dots of hot glue.

8 Glue the bottom of the spice bottle to the center of the bundt pan, and glue the feet of the doll to the lid. Then wrap the bottle with a piece of gold cardstock cut to fit around the bottle.

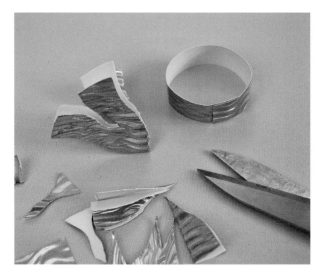

9 Now for the crown! Cut a strip of gold card about 6-inches long and ½-inch wide, make a circle of it, and glue the ends together. Cut a 5 x 5-inch square of gold card, fold it in half, and fold that in half again. Then make some cuts as shown. Make curved cuts on the sides, but leave the paper attached at the point for about a half inch. Then cut the flared shape out of the center. When you unfold it, you should have an eight-pointed asterisk shape. Save the scrap pieces.

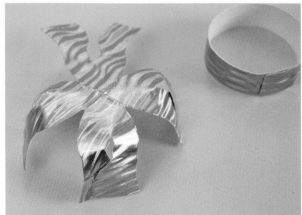

10 Unfold the card, and then overlap and glue the ends of every
second asterisk point together. Now put these ends down inside
the circle and glue them into place, evenly spaced around the
inside of the circle.

11 Finally, push down the center, push a piece
of scrap felt into the bottom, and glue the
center down to that. Now glue some scrap
pieces of gold back on, and glue the crown
to the doll's head.

12 Take a small piece of polymer clay, squish it flat, and cut out a tiny cross about a quarter-inch high, and bake it at 275° for 10 minutes. When finished baking, hot glue the cross to the top of a large blue marble, and paint the bands and cross in gold paint. Attach more trim and pom-poms if you like that kind of thing. For the last touch, put a couple of handfuls of red and gold florist's marbles in the bundt pan, stick all your lottery tickets in them, and place facing the door. Good luck!

LET THERE BE LIGHT SWITCHES

Doesn't it just seem like a miracle when we flip that little toggle and the Lord, through His miracle of electricity, turns darkness into light? Provided we paid the electric bill that month, of course. Now, with a little glue and ingenuity, and a handful of vintage holy cards, you can thank Jesus every day for inventing electricity—and add a touch of class to your home or trailer at the same time.

MATERIALS
Vintage holy cards—check eBay or your auntie's bedside table drawer
Light switch plates
Mod Podge or acrylic matte medium

TOOLS
Brush
Craft knife
Screwdriver

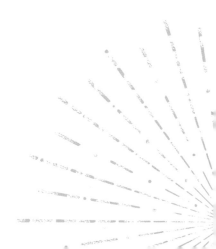

INSTRUCTIONS

1 Find some holy cards that have enough space in the middle to accommodate the hole for the switch. You can use your existing switch plates (but you'll need to take them off the wall first) or buy some new ones.

2 Brush some Mod Podge or acrylic matte medium on the back of the card and carefully position it on the switch plate, and smooth out.

3 When the Mod Podge has dried (about 15 minutes) turn the switch plate over. With a craft knife, carefully cut around the inside of the switch hole and remove the piece. Poke the knife tip through the bottom screw hole only. You really only need one screw to hold the switch plate in place, and the top screw will probably cover something important on the card anyway.

4 Now brush a coat or two of Mod Podge or acrylic medium on the front of the card. When it's dry, your switch plates are ready to go!

SMELLS LIKE HOLY SPIRIT PILLOWS

As I was doing my daily Bible reading, I came upon a passage in Ezekiel that gave me pause: "Wherefore thus saith the Lord God; Behold, I am against your pillows." I don't know if it meant He doesn't like them on principle, or if He is literally leaning against them. Either way, I took that as a sign that God was trying to tell me something that in my heart of hearts I already knew: That it's time to spruce up the flaccid sacks on Auntie's couch that she laughably calls "pillows." No amount of fluffing, no matter how strenuous, was ever going to revive them. So I took them out to the target range and put them out of their misery, then set about making some new ones. Now, when I sit down to watch my shows, I can lean back into the luxurious, heavenly smelling arms of Jesus.

MATERIALS

Some colored decorative rope, about a quarter-inch thick. You'll need about
   3 feet of rope for each pillow
3 satin pillowcases
A sheet of inkjet iron-on transfer paper
Pom-pom trim, about one yard
3 potpourri sachets

TOOLS

Lighter   Fabric glue
Pliers   Iron
Pencil   Inkjet printer

INSTRUCTIONS

1 I made three pillows—two with rope lettering, and one with an iron-on image of our Lord. Let's start with the lettering. First, use a lighter to melt the end of the rope slightly, and then squeeze the ends with pliers. This will keep it from unraveling.

2 Draw out your letters on the pillowcase with a contrasting pencil, using light marks.

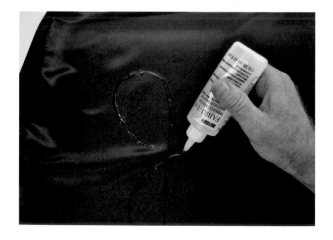

3 Lay down a generous bead of fabric glue along the lines. Work one letter or small section at a time.

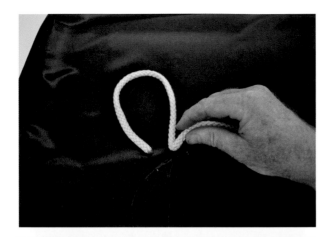

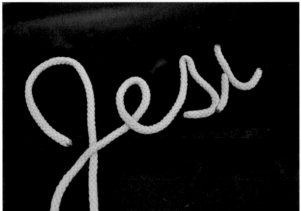

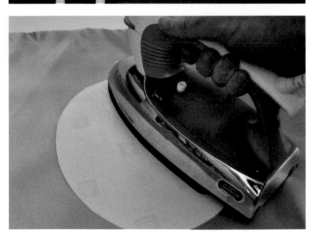

4 Lay down your rope. Then press it down firmly and give the glue a minute to set up before you move on.

5 The pink rope I used was silky Japanese bondage rope. Not that I'm into that (and if you are, I won't judge—I'll leave that to God) but it was just nice and thick, flexible, soft, and came in great colors. Since it was a little thicker than the gold rope I used for the other pillow, I decided it looked better to cut the rope rather than overlap it for some of the letters. If you do this, be sure to melt the ends of the rope as you go.

6 While the glue dries, you can work on the third pillowcase. Find a nice image of Our Savior. Size it so it will fill a letter-sized sheet, and print it on the transfer paper. Follow the manufacturer's instructions for printing and ironing. Glue the pom-pom trim around the outside of the image. When your cases are done, toss a potpourri sachet in each before you stuff in a pillow.

THY KINGDOM COME CANDLES

In this fast-paced world, sometimes it's hard to remember to pause to commune with the Lord. When you are too tired or busy, this beautiful candle will do the praying for you. Just light its gentle flame and the soft glow of faith will bring a sense of peace to any room, heal the sick, and help mask odors. Faith works miracles!

For this I used alginate mold material—if you haven't tried using it before to make molds, you're in for a treat. It's nontoxic, water based, and relatively idiot proof (individual results may vary). And fun! After you try it, you'll want to try casting all kinds of body parts.

MATERIALS
Alginate molding material, like Alja-Safe or Create-A-Mold
Cold water
1 candle wick, 6 inches long
Hot water
Soy candle wax flakes
Fragrance oil (optional)

TOOLS
Large bowl
Spatula
Gallon-sized plastic bucket or container
Pencil
Toothpicks
Medium saucepan
Large Pyrex measuring cup

INSTRUCTIONS

1 Get everything ready beforehand—alginate sets very fast, so you need to be prepared. Mix the alginate according to the directions. In a large bowl, add the powder and the right amount of *cold* water, and stir with a spatula. Pour the mixture into the bucket. Wet your hands, arrange them in a praying position, and insert them into the alginate. Hold in place until the mixture sets—usually about 2 minutes. When it feels firm, ease your hands out of the alginate. It's very flexible, so you should have no problem. If some mixture went between your hands, just pull it out. Now reach in and carefully clean up any stray bits of material left inside the mold. Let the mold sit for a couple of hours to get totally firm. Lay it on its side for a few minutes to drain out the extra water, but be careful not to dump the mold out of the container or it may break apart.

2 Now stick a wick down inside the mold. Use a pencil to push the wick into the alginate at the bottom. This will make sure it sticks out the top of your candle. Use a couple of toothpicks to support the wick so it's roughly in the middle of the candle.

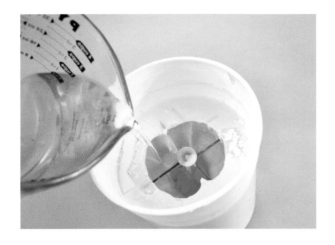

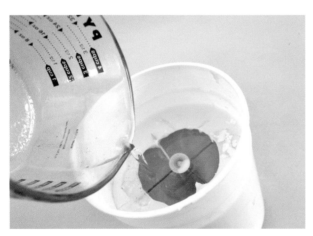

3 In a medium saucepan, heat up 2 cups of water until it's just about to boil. Then place about 4 cups of soy wax flakes in a large Pyrex measuring cup and set it in the hot water. When the wax starts to melt, turn off the stove. This is so you don't ignite the liquid wax and burn the trailer park to the ground—as so many novice candle makers before you have done, believe you me. If you want a scented candle, mix a little fragrance oil into the melted wax.

4 With alginate molds, it's better to build up a few layers of wax first, rather than cast it all at once. Fill your mold with wax, wait for a beat, and then pour the hot wax back out. This will coat the inside of the mold with a layer of wax. Give the first layer of wax a minute to cool, and then fill with hot wax again, and pour out and wait a minute again. By now, your patience has probably run out, so fill up the mold. Now give the candle at least an hour to fully cool, and then gently ease it out of the mold, and go find a pack of matches!

LET GO, LET GOD CURTAIN TIEBACK

When you crawl out of bed and throw open the curtains, let the baby Jesus help you greet the morning and marvel at the beauty of God's works. My window treatments have been on the receiving end of so many compliments since I swapped out my tired old secular tiebacks—a nail and a piece of twine—with these gorgeous faith-based ones. And they were so easy and fun to make! You could use colored or metallic paint to decorate them, but this is a good opportunity to brush up on your metal-leafing skills, and nothing beats the luster and shine of gold and copper leaf.

MATERIALS

Small metal Jell-O or chocolate molds

Metal leaf adhesive

Gold, copper, or variegated metal leaf

Paper plate

Brown acrylic paint

Spring and solid doorstops with hard rubber tips

Small baby Jesus figures from nativity scenes; you can find these on
   eBay or at flea markets

TOOLS

Icepick or nail

Soft brushes

Soft cloth

3/4-inch screws

Screwdriver

Hot glue gun

INSTRUCTIONS

1 Use the icepick to punch a hole in the center of the metal mold.

2 Clean the molds well, and then brush or spray on the metal leaf adhesive, following the manufacturer's instructions.

3 When the adhesive is tacky, brush on the gold leaf. Doing this part on a paper plate will make cleanup much easier. The variegated foil is a mix of copper, gold, and green flakes. You can just shake the flakes onto the adhesive and use the brush to flatten them into the adhesive.

4 For the smaller molds, I used pure copper leaf, which comes in sheets. To apply it, tear off small pieces, lay them onto the adhesive, and use the brush to push the foil into place and stick it down. Don't worry if there are gaps—you can put more small pieces on top to fill them. When you have the entire surface covered with foil, use the brush and a soft cloth to gently brush away the extra foil and smooth the surface.

5 For these smaller ones, I also wanted a darker background for the baby Jesus, so I brushed dark brown acrylic paint in the center.

6 Use the screw to attach the mold to the doorstop. Spring doorstops have a hard rubber tip which will hold the screw. Put some hot glue over the screw head to help hold it in place.

7 Hot glue the baby Jesus figure to the mold. Now you're ready to mount your tieback on the wall! Make a small pilot hole in the wall with the ice pick or a nail, and then screw in the doorstop.

GUARDIAN ANGEL BACKUP ROLL COZY

When you reach for the toilet paper, and find none, do you succumb to feelings of deep despair? Matthew tells us that during the Agony in the Garden, when Jesus was overcome with anguish and sadness at the thought of the torment and crucifixion that awaited him, an angel came down from heaven to comfort and strengthen him. Now you can have your own personal guardian angel—one that will always have a backup roll for you! Even better—she is kind enough to avert her gaze. Because—let's face it—there's something a little creepy about someone staring at you while you do your business, even if they are one of the Lord's messengers.

I made the angel using the body and head of one of Auntie's old dolls. After I removed the arms, legs, hair, and clothes, it was an easy matter to transform it into something beautiful.

MATERIALS

Small doll, about 7 inches in height

Tinfoil

Air-dry clay

Wooden plaque

Container that will fit over a roll of toilet paper, such as a flower pot or half-gallon food container

Ivory gloss spray paint

Gold paint or marker

TOOLS

Pencil or modeling tool

Sandpaper or wet sponge

Hot glue gun

INSTRUCTIONS

1 Remove the doll's arms, legs, and hair (if any) first.

2 Make long "ropes" of tinfoil, and push them through the arm and leg holes and bend them into the basic shapes of the arms and legs. You may need to jam extra pieces of foil in the holes to hold the foil arms in position.

3 Wrap the legs in a single flat piece of clay. Be sure to dampen the doll slightly before you stick on the clay— this will help it adhere. Smooth it with your fingers, and use the modeling tool to form the legs.

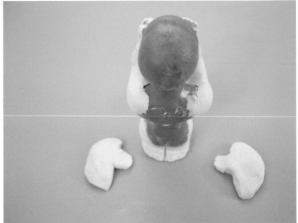

4 Working one section at a time, wrap the arms in a flat piece of clay and smooth and shape. It will be easier to work on the wings and hair if you let the arms and legs dry first. If your doll was bisque (ceramic) you can bake it at a low temp in the oven for a few minutes. If your doll is composition or plastic, use a hairdryer to speed up the drying, but be careful not to melt it.

5 Form two little kidney shapes out of clay for the wings, about 2 x 2 inches, as shown. The little tabs will attach to the shoulder blades. The wings will be stronger if you make sure the lowest point of the wing rests on the lower back for support.

6 Stick on the wings, smooth and shape them, and draw some lines to create the feathers with a modeling tool. Let them dry before you continue.

7 After I removed its hair, my doll had a bald lumpy head covered with old glue, so I made her a new hairdo out of clay.

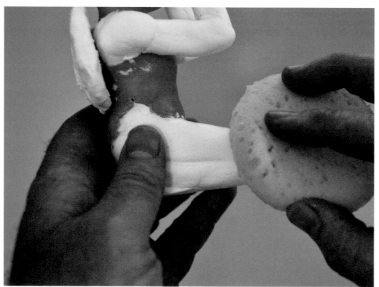

8 When the clay is thoroughly dried, you can carve and sand it. I prefer using a wet sponge for smoothing—it makes no dust, and it makes a thin paste of clay and water that will fill any cracks.

9 You could just stick your angel onto a container at this point, but a small wooden plaque makes a perfect little podium and gives it a more finished look. You can use any container that will work—a 2-quart food container, a flowerpot, a small basket. I found an old metal planter that was the perfect size for a backup toilet paper roll, after I dumped out the African violet that had previously occupied it. Use hot glue to attach the plaque to the bottom of the container, and then hot glue your angel onto that.

10 Spray it with several coats of ivory gloss spray paint. Build up thin coats until you have a nice thick glossy finish. For the final, perfect touch, highlight the edges of the podium with some gold.

EYE-SEE-YOU-IN-HELL MIRROR

Makes a great gift for your backslider friends! When they first see it, they'll be drawn to its elegant beauty and move in for a closer look, and then the all-seeing eye will hold them in its powerful hypnotic grip. Unable to look away, their gaze will fall down…down into the bloodred pupil, finally coming to rest upon their own reflection—magnified in the mirror, framed in fire, and giving them forewarning of their eternal torments in hell. When they see their bloated sinful faces, the shame and fear might drive them to take a big ole page from your book and attend church every Sunday!

MATERIALS

2 pieces of 1½-inch florist's Styrofoam—a 12 x 18-inch rectangle, and a 9-inch circle

Small circular magnifying shaving/makeup mirror, about 5 inches across

2 tubes of latex window glazing putty

Small putty knife or spatula

Blue and white sea glass, shells, beads, buttons, charms, marbles and/or rhinestones

Letter beads

Red florist's marbles

TOOLS

Marker

Small saw

Dust mask

Rasp

Caulking gun (If you don't have one, you can cut open the tubes with a knife.)

Glue

INSTRUCTIONS

1 Measure and mark the halfway points on each side of the Styrofoam rectangle, draw an eye shape that fills the whole 12 x 18-inch piece of foam, and cut it out with the saw. A dust mask is a good idea when cutting and shaping the foam, or you'll be coughing up foam dust for days.

2 Use the rasp to round off the square edges and shape the foam pieces.

3 Put the mirror in the center of the eye and draw around it with a marker, then cut out the center. Mark and cut that circle out of the other piece of foam—this will be the pupil. Glue the "iris" onto the eye, being sure to line up the holes. Then squeeze some putty onto a paper plate and start spreading it on the foam and placing your shell and glass bits. Start with the letter beads, and do a small area at a time, doing the "white" of the eye first.

4 Next, set the mirror into the bottom of the hole. Don't affix it yet. Now spread some putty on the inside of the hole and set the red florist's marbles. When you're done, clean off any putty you got on the marbles.

5 Now work on the "iris," spreading putty and setting your blue glass pieces and shells on the raised circular part of the eye. Set the eye where it can sit undisturbed for a couple of days for the putty to fully set. Lastly, take the mirror out of the back and clean it, and then glue it back in place. Now you're ready to place the eye where the gaze of a sinner might fall upon it!

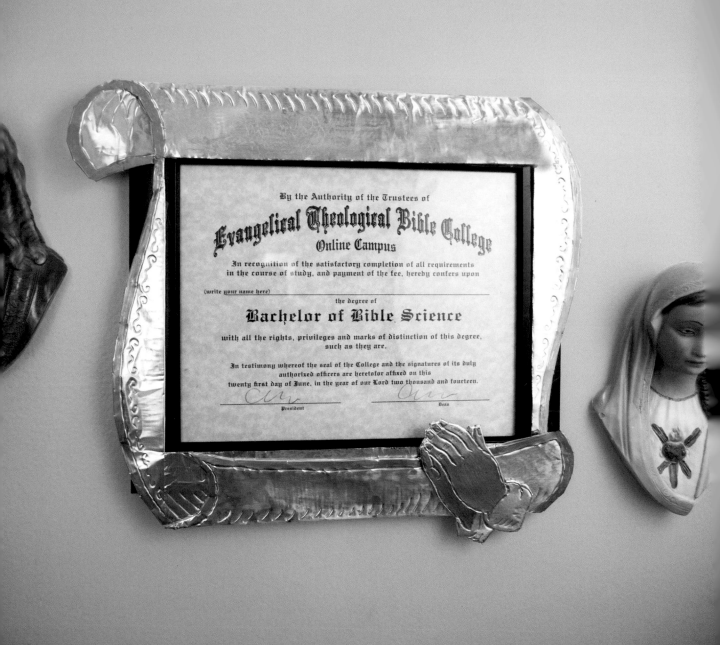

By the Authority of the Trustees of

Evangelical Theological Bible College
Online Campus

In recognition of the satisfactory completion of all requirements
in the course of study, and payment of the fee, hereby confers upon

(write your name here)

the degree of

Bachelor of Bible Science

with all the rights, privileges and marks of distinction of this degree,
such as they are.

In testimony whereof the seal of the College and the signatures of its duly
authorized officers are heretofor affixed on this
twenty first day of June, in the year of our Lord two thousand and fourteen.

_____   _____
President   Dean

PRECIOUS METAL DIPLOMA FRAME

If you have a favorite Bible verse you'd like to frame, or your diploma from the online Evangelical Theological College, you won't want a normal boring diploma frame from the local big box store. Proper framing requires thoughtful planning and consideration, not to mention a good eye for design. To make a piece of art look its best, a good frame should complement, as well as subtly enhance. Professional framing can be too cost prohibitive, though. Luckily I have come up with an affordable alternative that is a piece of art in and of itself. It has the look of beautiful silverwork, tipped with gilt, all at a fraction of the price!

You could use embossing foil for this, but I had some foil tape lying around, and that stuff is very thick and strong, and the adhesive sticks like hell. Be careful handling the cut edges—it can also cut like hell, and no craft is worth bleeding out over. Don't worry if you can only find foil tape with manufacturer's logos printed on it—the printing is easily removed with lighter fluid.

MATERIALS
2 or 3 pieces of craft foam, 9 x 12 inches
6 or 7 feet of aluminum foil repair tape, 2½ inches wide
Diploma frame

TOOLS
Masking tape
Pencil
Craft knife or scissors
Hot glue gun
Fine steel wool or a scouring pad
Gold marker

INSTRUCTIONS

1 Measure and cut the craft foam. You'll need two 12 x 12-inch pieces, two 9.5 x 1.5-inch pieces, and two 12-inch-long pieces that taper from 3 inches wide to 2 inches on the other end. Lay them out as shown. Put a piece of tape on each seam, and flip it over. Use a pencil to draw the curved sides as shown, and then cut them with the knife or scissors.

2 Lay the tapered pieces on top of the bottom edge, and under the top edge as shown, and draw the curves as shown. Cut those out as well. Now you will cover the fronts of the pieces with the foil tape.

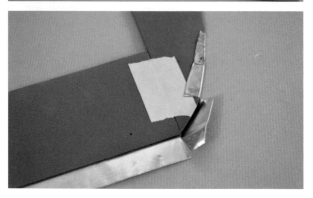

3 Peel the backing paper off the aluminum tape and lay the strips along the long pieces of craft foam. Trim any extra tape with the scissors, leaving about a half inch extra, which you will fold over the edge and back. For the curved edges, cut regular slits as shown, and then bend each tab over one at a time. Then smooth the edges with the pencil or your fingernail to remove any bumps.

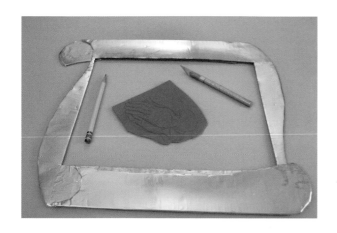

4 When the pieces are covered with foil tape, hot glue them together. On another piece of craft foam about 3 x 3 inches, draw the praying hands. You can use a pattern for this if you need to. Press the pencil lines fairly deep into the foam.

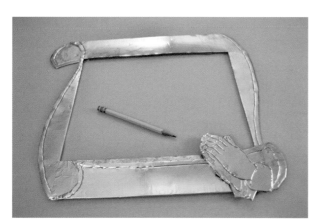

5 Now cut out the hands, and cover the front with foil tape, and trim, leaving a half inch extra border. Make little tabs to bend around the curves like you did with the larger pieces. If you rub down the tape on the front, your deep pencil lines will show up. Using them as a guide, press lines into the foil with the pencil tip. Do the same with the edges of the frame, to add a border to the scroll. Then hot glue the hands to the bottom of the frame. Clean the foil and buff it with fine steel wool or a scouring pad to remove any marks. Use the gold marker to accent the border and hands with gold. Now line up the finished foil frame with your diploma frame and hot glue it down.

LIGHT-OF-LIFE WALL SCONCE

Lighting can help set the mood in any room. If the mood you are going for is one of hushed reverence, then you can't go wrong with a couple of these elegant wall sconces. Let the Lord light up your life with a soft peaceful glow that will also be plenty enough light to see the buttons on the remote. The shades are paper—you could just use colored or patterned paper if you wanted a more secular feel, but to hell with that. I found some old calendars that Auntie had saved, with beautiful vintage graphics on them. I knew I had to find a use for them. And by the way—who saves old calendars?

MATERIALS

Two 8½ x 11-inch images of your choosing, in landscape format

Matte or soft gloss photo paper, or other good quality cardstock

4-foot piece of 1-inch lath. (It's a long skinny piece of wood—ask the nice man at the hardware store.)

2 snap-in light socket kits and LED candelabra bulbs. (DO NOT use regular candelabra bulbs, which will get too hot and may burn the paper shade.)

Double-sided foam mounting tape

TOOLS

Scanner and printer

8-inch wooden embroidery hoop

Utility knife

Small saw

Hot glue gun

2 pairs of needle-nose pliers

WARNING: *When you go to the hardware store and see the price on the LED bulbs, you'll want to cheap out with every fiber of your being, and buy the regular bulbs. When you get this feeling, and you will, just picture your mug shot in the newspaper, under the headline "Cheapskate burns down neighborhood to save $4. Death toll 253 and rising," and the feeling should go away. The regular bulbs, even dim ones, are too hot for this light and shade—it'll go up like the Hindenburg. The LED bulbs throw great light, don't get hot, use almost no power, and last nearly forever. Use 'em!*

INSTRUCTIONS

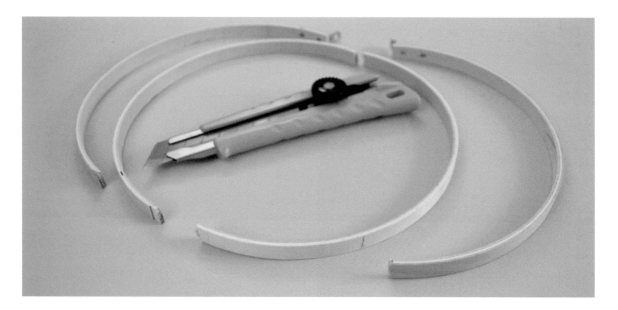

1 Your first job is to find 2 images you like. You can find them online, or scan any postcard, calendar, or Sunday school good-attendance card that strikes your fancy. If it's already 8½ x 11 inches in landscape format and a fairly high quality, then you are good to go. Otherwise you will need to resize it. If you don't know how, any teenager can probably help. Print them out at a good quality setting on the best quality cardstock or photo paper you can find. If your printer can do it, print them borderless. If not, your shade will have a white border— not the end of the world. While the prints dry, separate the 2 rings of your embroidery hoop, then measure and cut them in half. The wood is very soft, so the utility knife will work. Pull off the 2 metal tabs with pliers.

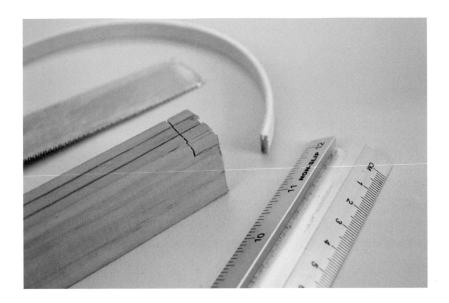

2 Now measure and cut the lath with the small saw. You need 4
   pieces that are 8½ inches long, and 2 pieces that are 6¾ inches
   long. Now you need to cut little notches in both ends of the
   long pieces, the width and thickness of the hoop pieces. The
   hoop will sit in those notches. So stack the four longer pieces,
   and line up the ends. Then mark the width of the hoop, hold
   them firmly in one hand, and make a cut with the saw, as
   shown, through all 4 pieces at once.

3 Use the utility knife to make the other cut,
   along the wood grain, and pop out the little
   piece of wood to finish the notch. If you
   have a chisel for this, it's easier.

4 Now to finish the paper shade part. By sheer coincidence, the hoop halves will each be almost exactly 11 inches long, so we'll be gluing them down along the long edges of our prints, to form a big half-cylinder shape. Quickly run a thin bead of hot glue along the outside of the hoop half. Now quickly line it up in the corner, and roll it down along the paper, keeping it lined up with the edge. If you don't feel you can work quickly enough, you can try gluing along the edge as you roll down the hoop with your other hand. Apply a very thin line of glue—too much will blob out of the edges. When the glue is hard, trim the ends of the hoop with the utility knife so they line up with the edge of the paper.

5 Now place 2 long pieces of wood on your work surface with the notches pointing out. Lay the shade on them and line everything up so the notches fit into the hoop ends. Hold the wood pieces down firmly with one hand, and lift off the paper shade, trying not to move the wood pieces. If you're having trouble with this, try taping the wood pieces in place before removing the shade.

6 While still holding the wood firmly down, put 2 blobs of hot glue in the middle of each, and then stick the shorter piece of wood down. Hold firmly for a couple of seconds until it hardens. You now have a big wood capital H!

7 Take the socket and use the pliers to bend one of the metal tabs flat. Glue the flat tab to the middle of the crossbar. You want the little socket to point straight up and down, not at a jaunty angle.

8 You're ready to glue on your shade! Run a thin bead of glue along one outside edge of the H, and stick the ends of the hoops and the edges of the paper shade in place. Do the same thing on the other side.

9 Put a strip of foam mounting tape on the back of each vertical stick, and mount the lights to the wall.

TIME-TO-OBEY-THE-LORD CLOCK

We all know the power of the prayers of a righteous person to heal and change lives. As Mark so eloquently put it: "Whatever you ask in prayer, believe that you have received it, and it will be yours."

But sometimes in this fast-paced modern world we can forget to take the time to pray to the Lord. Have you been doing enough praying lately? Probably not, but there's no time like the present. Literally—put down the book and pray right now. There—doesn't that feel better? If you need a reminder, here is a clock that will give you one every time you check the time.

MATERIALS

Basswood round, ¾ inches thick
   and 9 x 11 inches oblong
Gel wood stain
Large paint stir stick, the kind the hardware
   store gives out with gallons of paint
2 jumbo-sized popsicle sticks or tongue depressors
White cardstock or heavy paper
Watercolor paint, markers, or colored pencils
Glue—white glue and heavy-duty craft glue
Water-based polyurethane or gloss acrylic glaze
Quartz clock motor, with a ¾-inch shaft
Gold paint or a gold marker
Small piece of wood or rigid foam

TOOLS

Pencil
Craft knife
Wax paper
Drill with 5/16ths bit
Small saw
Ruler
Fine waterproof black
   marker

INSTRUCTIONS

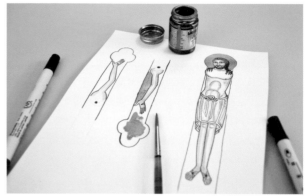

1 Basswood is very pale, so use a light coat of water-based transparent stain in a golden oak or maple color, then set aside to dry.

2 With a pencil, trace around the outside of the stir stick and the tongue depressors on the piece of card. Now draw Christ's arms on the card as shown—you want one to be longer for the minute hand. Draw His body and head on the larger outline of the large stir stick. You can draw yours freehand, or you could trace your favorite crucifix. I used a thirteenth-century icon as inspiration for mine. Color with watercolor, markers, or colored pencils. Paint around the outside with gold paint or marker.

3 Cut out the pieces with a craft knife, and glue them onto the sticks with white glue. Put them face down on a piece of wax paper, and place a large book or other weight on them and leave to dry.

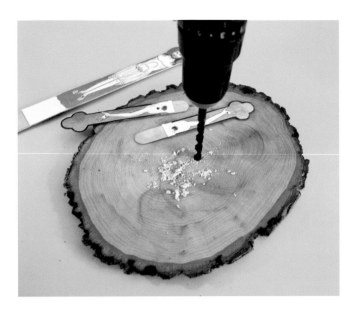

4 When they are dry, position the 3 pieces on the
basswood. Lift off the body piece, hold down the
arms, and carefully drill through them and into
the basswood. Once you have the hole started in
the basswood, back the drill out, remove the arm
pieces, and then finish drilling right through the
basswood.

5 Carefully trim off the ends of the three
sticks with the small saw.

6 Use a ruler and square to mark the 12 hours on the face. Draw very light pencil guidelines.

7 Use a fine waterproof black marker to letter the hours as shown. I used a blackletter font for mine. Then coat the basswood with one or two coats of water-based polyurethane or acrylic gloss and let dry for about 4 hours.

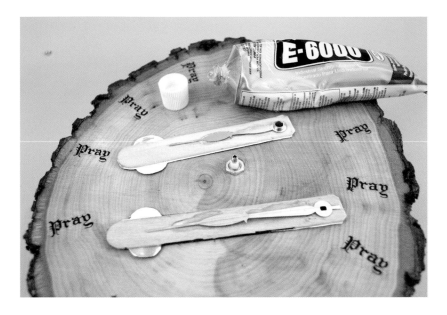

8 Position the hour and minute hands that came with your clock motor so their holes line up with the holes you drilled in the stir stick arms, and glue in place with heavy glue. I used E-6000 because it's strong and dries very fast.

9 Push the clock motor shaft through the hole, and screw down the nut on the shaft to hold it in place. Then put on the hands—hour first, then minute, and screw down the retaining nut. Then glue the small piece of wood down at the bottom, first making sure the minute hand will clear it. Glue the larger body piece to the small piece of wood, and clamp until the glue dries. If you do it right, Christ's body will float above the clock face, leaving enough room for the hands to pass by underneath.

EAT AND DRINK IN THE GLORY

Whether therefore ye eat, or drink, or whatsoever ye do, do all to the glory of God.

1 Corinthians 10:31

JESUS' PET DINOSAUR NACHO PLATTER

As everyone knows (those few of us who haven't fallen for that foolish theory nonsense!), the Bible tells us—I'm sure it's in there somewhere—that before the flood dinosaurs and men cohabited. A wise old homeless gentleman they call the "Preacher" told me that they've even found footprints of men and dinosaurs together in the same fossilized mud. Explain that, "Science"!

I like to think that old Noah left just enough room on his little arc to save one or two dino eggs from the rising waters to give to the Lord's son to raise as pets. And I'm not going to let some godless Poindexter scientist tell me I'm wrong! I'm going to celebrate their friendship with this lovely 3-D diorama platter rest!

Now, when I get to the pearly gates, Saint Peter might ask me why in God's name I put Our Savior on a brontosaurus and not a T-Rex. Well, I did pray on it, and the Lord spoke to me. Jesus told me that he was the Prince of Peace, not the Prince of bloodthirsty killing machines.

This craft will call upon your polymer clay sculpting skills. To make life easier, I used a bake-as-you-go method of building the dinosaur and Jesus. First you form and bake the body, then attach one or two limbs, bake again, and so on.

MATERIALS

Tinfoil, about 3 feet

Polymer clay, about 8 ounces

Wire, about 2 feet (Armature wire works best, but soft iron wire would, too.)

Piece of heavy cardboard

Green acrylic paint

12-inch plastic plate, blue looks best

16-inch party platter

Can of spray foam insulation, minimal expansion

Spray paint—a can of pale green, and a can of brushed bronze

Some plastic plants and moss

Jump ring and black silk cord (optional)

TOOLS

Wire nippers   Sandpaper

Baking sheet   Small saw or serrated bread knife

Pencil or modeling tool   Hot glue gun

INSTRUCTIONS

1 Take a 12 x 18-inch piece of tinfoil and scrunch it up and form into a flattened teardrop shape about 5 inches long, and 2 inches wide at its widest point. Flatten it so it's about ¾-inches thick.

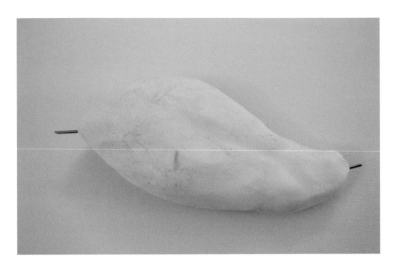

2 Cover the teardrop with a layer of clay about a quarter inch thick, and stick a 1-inch piece of wire in each end. Bake this at 275° for about ten minutes.

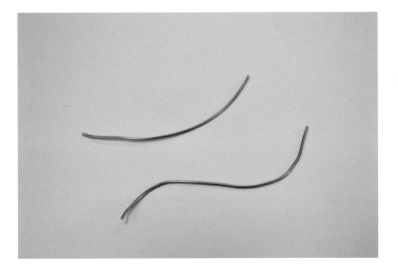

3 Cut 2 pieces of wire about 3 inches long, and shape one into a slight curve, and the other into a lazy-S shape as shown.

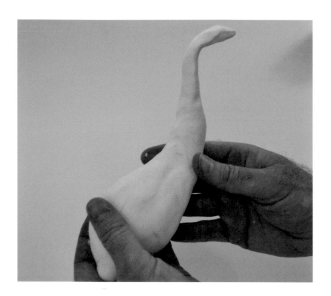

4 Apply clay around the S-shaped wire to make the neck and head as shown. Apply it to the body. Use a pencil tip or other tool to make the face details. Now bake the neck and body. Repeat the process with the tail.

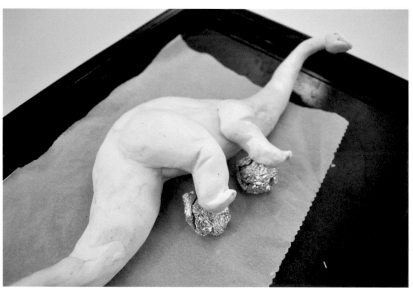

5 Now make a front and back leg. Place the body on a baking sheet, and place 2 balls of tinfoil under the legs to hold them in position while it's baking.

6 Now position the dinosaur upright, and hot glue his feet to a piece of heavy cardboard. This will hold him in position while you make and bake his other 2 legs. This is also a good time to fill any cracks or dents with clay.

7 Let's get started on Jesus. Make a little stick man out of pieces of wire and a tinfoil body. Sit him on the dinosaur and bend him until you get a position that looks good.

8 Now cover the head and body with clay. Add some details to the face and some wrinkles to his robe with the pencil point, and then bake. Now build him up in stages like you did with the dino—add arms and bake, then lower legs, and finally hair and robe details. You can harden the thin layers of clay with a heat gun rather than baking.

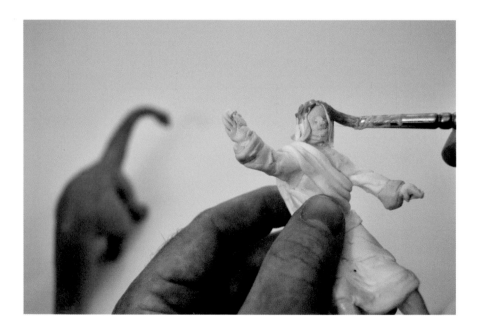

9 Now finish by sanding the dinosaur smooth and painting him green with acrylic paint. While he's drying, paint the details on our Lord.

10 Place the plate on the platter so it is off center. Spray the foam insulation onto the platter until you build up a nice little hill, and let it harden for a half hour or so.

11 When it's hard, cut off the top with a small saw or serrated bread knife to make a flat plateau for the dino to stand on. Spray paint the foam and platter pale green. When that's dry, spray with the bronze. Let the green show through in the gaps. This will give the rocks a natural moss-covered look.

12 Now it's just a matter of figuring out a pleasing arrangement of greenery and gluing everything together with the hot glue gun. You can also stick some fake plant stems right into the foam. For the final touch, make a little collar out of a scrap of craft foam and a jump ring, and a leash out of black silk cord.

LAST SUPPER LUNCH BOX

Sadly, I decided it was time to retire my Flintstones lunch box, which had served me faithfully since grade school. I think it was sending the wrong message to my colleagues at the plant, and was the only reason I could think of that I was passed over for a promotion every year. Its replacement was sturdy but bland, so some decoupage was in order. I found a beautiful reproduction of DaVinci's Last Supper in one of Auntie's art books that was a perfect fit, but she strongly objected when she spied me cutting it out. She puts up quite a fight for someone who looks like a plus-sized Crypt Keeper! Luckily I was able to find a good copy online, and added some vintage holy cards that I knew the old hoarder would never miss.

Now, when I walk into the lunchroom with a skip in my step, my new lunch box lets everyone know I'm a team player. And who knows—it just might boost employee morale!

MATERIALS

Metal dome-top lunch box
Vintage holy cards (you can find these on eBay.)
Mod Podge
Gold paint marker
Acrylic gloss glaze

TOOLS

Ruler
Craft knife
Inkjet or laser printer
Circle cutter
Brush

INSTRUCTIONS

1 Measure the panels of your lunch box. Measure, print, and cut the *Last Supper* painting to fit the large horizontal front panel on the dome lid of the lunch box. Find some holy cards that work and decide on the placement.

2 I used a circle cutter to cut up some of the cards so they fit better and looked more interesting. I also cut rounded tops on 2 cards for the ends of the dome top. Now brush Mod Podge on the back of your paper pieces and press them into place.

3 There is nothing that can't be made prettier with a little gold paint—nothing. So when the Mod Podge is dry, use a gold paint marker to add some decorative frames and ornaments. Use a light touch—you don't want this to be too gaudy. Now seal the front and edges of the paper with a coat of Mod Podge. It isn't waterproof, so when it's dry, finish your lunch box with a good coat of acrylic gloss glaze. Now the only thing missing is a couple of baloney sandwiches and a thermos of milk!

GOBLETS OF HIS GLORY

Turn old jars into elegant glassware worthy of toasting Our Savior! Whether you sip, quaff, or chug, these good-looking glasses will fill you with the Holy Spirit faster than Jesus turned water into wine! You could go buy some mason jars, but if you have friends with gardens, you probably have dusty shelves full of unwanted gifts of their pickles and jams and other strange preserves of dubious provenance. In my case, I snagged a few store-bought food jars from the trash, and I dumped out a few jars of Auntie's favorite sweet-and-sour pickles, which I could never abide.

MATERIALS
Some jars
Lighter fluid
Heavy paper stock
Acrylic transfer medium (I like Omni-Gel.)
Bowl of water
Paper towels
Some stained glass images of Jesus from books or the Internet

TOOLS
Laser printer or waterproof inkjet printer
Brush
Hairdryer or heat gun
Scissors

INSTRUCTIONS

1 Remove the jar labels by soaking in warm water. Remove any leftover label glue with lighter fluid. Wash the jars well with soap and water. Now find some images you like. I searched online for some beautiful stained glass windows of Our Savior. Measure the jars, and print your images to size. I find heavy paper stock works best for this. Matte photo paper works well, and the colors print brighter and sharper. Use a laser printer or a waterproof inkjet printer. If you don't have either, try spraying ordinary inkjet prints with a couple of coats of fixative, which will keep the inks from running when you brush on the transfer medium.

2 Brush the transfer medium on the prints. I like Omni-Gel medium. It's tougher than Mod Podge, and more importantly it dries completely waterproof. Brush on 3 good coats of medium, letting it dry thoroughly between coats. Brush the first coat on horizontally, and the next coat vertically, etc. You can speed up the drying time with a hairdryer or heat gun.

3 Soak your prints in water for at least 30 minutes. Then pick at the edge of the print until you start to lift the coat of medium, which is now dried into a flexible film. Very gently peel them apart. If the paper starts to tear, put it back in the water and try again. Any leftover bits of paper can be rewetted and rubbed off the back. Your image is now a thin translucent film—it's almost miraculous! Pat it dry between paper towels.

4 Trim your image with scissors. Place it shiny side down on some newspaper and brush a coat of transfer medium on the back, and rub it down onto the jar with a paper towel. Quickly remove any extra medium from the glass with a damp paper towel. While waiting for it to dry, mix up a batch of adult lemonade!

DAILY BREAD PLATES

Saying grace before meals is a time to reflect upon how thankful we should be for God's bounty. But as we enjoy the meal that God has provided with His Grace, let us also remember that it isn't always easy to be a Christian. This is a good time to remind your friends that many of us have been persecuted and tortured for our faith. Most often by other Christians, but that's a talk for another time. What better way to honor their memory, and make mealtime a teachable moment, than with these plates covered with beautiful paintings of these martyrs? After your guests dig down through the spaghetti and get a gander at what's been hiding under their food, they will be praying, but it won't be for seconds. No, it's not your cooking; they won't want to cover up those beautiful images again!

MATERIALS

Plastic party plates

Images of Christian martyrdom (The Internet is loaded with them.)

High-quality printer paper

Mod Podge

Red acrylic paint or alcohol ink

Acrylic gloss varnish

TOOLS

Laser printer or inkjet printer with waterproof ink

Compass

Scissors or craft knife

Fine sanding pad

Brushes

INSTRUCTIONS

1 Measure your plates, and then size your images and print. I used satin photo paper and an inkjet printer that prints waterproof images. You can also use a laser printer. Use a compass to mark a circle on each print and then cut out with scissors or a craft knife.

2 Sand the centers of your plates with a fine sanding pad, otherwise the Mod Podge won't stick. Brush on a layer of Mod Podge, position your circle print, and press down. Brush out any wrinkles or air bubbles and let dry.

3 I felt the original painters of these masterpieces skimped a bit on the blood. Maybe red paint was more expensive in the Renaissance. No matter—some bloodred alcohol ink fixed that.

4 I also applied a simple yet elegant border with the red ink. Finally, brush on 2 or 3 coats of the acrylic varnish. While they dry, you can start cooking up a meal and invite over all your friends!

KEEP
CHRIST
IN
CHRISTMAS

MAY
CHRIST
BE WITH
YOU

MERRY
CHRIST
MAS

FIRST CLASS MAIL

IT'S CHRISTMAS, FOR CHRIST'S SAKE!

And when they were come into the house, they saw the young child with Mary his mother, and fell down, and worshiped him: and when they had opened their treasures, they presented unto him gifts, gold, and frankincense, and myrrh.

—Matthew 2:11

SANTA CLAUS IS COMING TO TOWN NATIVITY SCENE

Just like you and everyone else on Earth, I rejoice every Christmas at the birth of Our Savior, but something about the Bible story always held a tinge of sadness for me. I think it was the fact that the little baby Jesus never got to see what a great holiday his birthday turned into. He never got to fall asleep on Christmas Eve dreaming about old Saint Nick, or come down the stairs on Christmas morning and see the tree twinkling with lights and beautiful ornaments. He never got to feel the thrill of unwrapping all his presents and looking into his stocking, stuffed with goodies. The closest he got was the gifts of the three so-called "wise" men. I mean, who brings a little kid incense for a Christmas present!? So I decided it was time to set things right, and create a vision of the perfect first Christmas, the way it should have been.

MATERIALS

Craft felt, 9 x 12-inch sheet of white,
  red, yellow, brown, green, light and
  dark blue, and light and dark green
Heavy-duty glue, like E-6000 or
  Beacon Quick Grip
White glue
Red 3-inch Christmas ornament
Small piece of black craft foam,
  a 2 x 2-inch scrap will be plenty
Colored pipe cleaners
3/4-inch bead or ball
Pale pink or flesh-colored paint
Cotton balls
Red stickpin

Gold cardstock
Ribbon
Wood clothespins
Colored yarn and twine
Acrylic paint or markers
3 gold beads
Small birdhouse, about 6 x 8
  inches
Dried straw

TOOLS

Small saw
Hot glue gun
Utility knife

INSTRUCTIONS

1 Cut some ¼-inch strips of white felt for Santa's suit, one about 9 inches long, the other about 2 inches long. Glue the long one around the red ornament, just below the middle. Glue a second strip from that first one up to the neck—the part of the ornament where the hanger is placed.

2 Now cut some pieces of red felt
1 x 1½ inches long. Cut one end slightly
rounded. Now cut some half-inch squares
of the black foam, and snip them into 4 little
feet, and 4 mittens. Finally, cut some strips
of white felt about ¼ inch wide x 1½ inches
long, and snip and bend some pipe cleaners.

3 The arms and legs are made the same way: Snip the
pipe cleaner to length—about 2 inches—and glue it
onto a boot (or mitten) and piece of red felt as shown.
Glue another boot or mitten on top of the first, then
fold over and glue the 2 sides of the red felt.

4 When they are dry, bend and glue them as shown. Remove the top of the ornament and glue a ¾-inch bead or ball to the neck and paint it pale pink or flesh colored. Then flatten out a cotton ball and glue to the chin as Santa's beard, and another one around the back of the neck for hair. Give him a red stickpin nose. Make a small cone out of a 3 x 3-inch piece of red felt, cut to size, and trim with white felt and glue in place. To make Santa's present, fold and tape some gold cardstock to make a 1-inch cube, wrap it in ribbon, and glue between Santa's hands.

5 For the other figures, we'll use clothespins for the bodies. First paint the faces onto the heads and let dry. Then cut a 3-inch square of felt, and then trim the sides as shown.

6 Wrap and glue the felt, trim if needed, and wrap a belt of yarn or pipe cleaner. The arms are made the same way as Santa's, only with pipe cleaner hands instead of mittens.

7 For Mary and the wise men, glue a small piece of different colored felt down the front, and make the robe less wide. Glue on the arms. Cut pieces of twine or yarn for hair and beards, and glue and trim. Then give them string headbands and draw on the faces with markers. Make the wise men's crowns out of strips of gold cardstock, and glue a gold bead between their hands for a present.

8 Use a saw to cut down the center of the birdhouse, and pry off one side of the roof, and the front and side walls as shown. Save the extra pieces of wood to make a manger for baby Jesus.

9 Trim the piece of roof you removed as shown, and glue it to the floor with a hot glue gun.

10 Spread white glue on the floor, and place some dried grass or straw on it. (Hamster bedding is also good.) While it dries, cut out a star from gold cardstock. I used 3 different colors of cardstock, and stuck them to each other with foam tape.

11 For the baby Jesus, saw the top off of a clothespin, paint the head, and swaddle it in pieces of white felt. Make him two arms out of a pink pipe cleaner. Use the utility knife to cut quarter-inch strips from the extra birdhouse wood, and glue them together to make a manger. Glue in a few pieces of dried grass, then glue baby Jesus into the manger. Finally, glue everyone in place and add any finishing touches.

WAR-ON-CHRISTMAS ACTION FIGURES

Every winter the media, government, retailers, and schools declare all-out war on Christmas and conspire to censor the birth of Jesus Christ. I do my part to counter the attack by shrieking "Merry CHRISTmas!" directly into the face of every Walmart greeter who wishes me "Happy holidays."

Well, if it's war, I know just the guys to fight it. Matthew mentions the Magi bringing gifts to baby Jesus, but he doesn't say who they are. Christian scholars have mulled it over for centuries, but can't agree. I figure my guess is as good as theirs, and I say it was none other than Shadrach, Meshach, and Abednego. You probably remember the Sunday school story about how king Nebuchadnezzar tossed them in a furnace for refusing to bow down to his statue. But when old Nebby looked in, not only were they not burned up, they were chilling with an angel in the roaring flames, as cool as cucumbers. I can't think of anyone better to fight the false god of Seasons Greetings than these Old Testament badasses and the Archangel Michael. You do NOT want to wish these guys a happy Kwanzaa!

No matter how many times I tell my coworkers that action figures are NOT kids' toys but adult collectibles, they still keep telling me to stop playing with dolls. Most of mine are still in their boxes to protect their value, but I did have a few spares that were good makeover candidates for this craft. But if you don't have any, you can usually find bins of them at yard sales or flea markets. Look for the higher-end ones with flexible joints.

MATERIALS

Four 7-inch action figures
Some small pieces of fabric, cardstock,
   faux leather, and craft fur
Several buttons and studs
Gold and black cords

TOOLS

Utility knife, scissors
Glue
Pen, markers
Paintbrushes

1 The first step is to give your action figures some Old Testament robes. Cut a small piece of fabric, roughly 4 x 6 inches, and glue it around the waist. I gave one figure a shoulder strap for his robe. Then cut a piece of cardstock or faux leather and wrap and glue it as a belt.

2 The hair and beards on some of my figures were all wrong, so I trimmed and glued craft fur, and gave them shoelace headbands. Now they have more of an Old Testament/Duck Dynasty look. I also used some waterproof markers to give them chest tattoos. My three weeks in cosmetology school was time well spent, despite what Auntie says.

3 Add final details—button and stud belt buckles, armbands, the ripped-off heads of secular humanists, etc.

4 My Archangel Michael figure had an ugly onesie so I painted it white.

5 For Archangel Michael's wings, fold a piece of white craft foam, trace a wing design on it about 3 x 6 inches, and cut out both sides at once with scissors.

6 Draw another set of wings that is just slightly smaller than the ones you just cut out. Cut out the smaller set of wings and attach to the larger set as another layer of feathers. Brush the tips with gold.

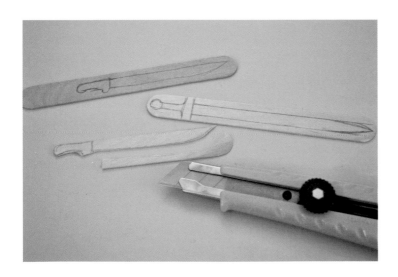

7 Draw the shapes of their swords on the tongue depressors, cut out with the utility knife, and then paint silver and gold.

A CHRISTMAS WISH

COUNT YOUR BLESSINGS
CARD DISPLAY

This is a classic Christmas craft, given a much-needed update. When I was a kid, we made these in Sunday school using old tomato juice cans and unwanted yarn. They were a little sad looking, and every year I couldn't wait for them to fill up with Christmas cards so I didn't have to look at them anymore. Luckily, these days we have a much wider variety of crafting materials to choose from. Now we're able to craft something that looks like what you might get if you mated a disco ball and a church hat, and will make you smile away those Christmas blues every time you see it, even if no one ever sends you any Christmas cards anymore!

MATERIALS
2 large cans with tops and bottoms removed
Fluffy yarn
Gold cord
Metallic foil mesh craft tubing
LED fairy lights

TOOLS
Can opener

INSTRUCTIONS

1 Use a can opener to remove the bottoms of the cans.

2 Decide which two cords or yarns you would like to wrap your cans with. I used 2 colors of metallic foil mesh craft tubing on one can, and fuzzy yarn and gold cord on another. If you are using 2 cords of different thicknesses, start with the thickest one. Pass the yarn or cord through the can, tie it to itself with a slipknot, and pull it tight.

3 Now simply pass the cord or yarn around and around the can, in and out, until you wrap it up. Leave some space between each strand. You'll need to always hold the cord tight against the edge of the can with one hand to keep tension on it. Try to maintain the same tension on every pass. When you get back to the beginning, tie off the end of the cord inside the can. Now take a second, contrasting color yarn or cord and tie the end to the first cord somewhere on the inside of the can where it won't be seen. Now wrap it around the can between the strands of the first color.

4 You can alternate strands of color, or do 1 strand of your second color to every 2 or 3 strands of your first—experiment until you get something that makes you happy. When you are using the gold cord, if you wrap it around a small bottle, as shown below, it will make it more manageable.

5 Finally, wrap the LED fairy lights around the can. When you place it on your mantle or centerpiece, conceal the battery pack inside. As you get Christmas cards, slide them under the strands, so that the cord rests against the middle fold of the card. You may want to save some cards every year so your friends think you get more than they do.

KEEP CHRIST IN CHRISTMAS

MAY CHRIST BE WITH YOU

MERRY CHRIST MAS

FIRST CLASS MAIL

COME ALL YE FAITHFUL CHRISTMAS CARDS

You might think the War on Christmas has a propaganda arm when you scan the Christmas card rack at your local store. You can find lots of Santas and snowmen and "Seasons Greetings," and very little scripture. It truly saddens yet enrages me. These cards are easy to make and so beautiful that the grateful recipients will want to save them as keepsakes. But most important, they'll remind all those "X-mas" "Happy Holidays" fools on your Christmas card list whose birthday it really is, anyway.

We're going to use a combination of two printing methods to do these cards—stenciling and rubber-stamping.

MATERIALS

Fun Foam stick-on craft letters

Spray adhesive

2 pieces of scrap wood about the size of a card, roughly 4 x 5 inches. (Pieces of foam core will work in a pinch.)

Sheet of copy paper

Piece of clear flexible plastic about 4 x 6 inches—the flat top of a clear plastic egg carton is perfect

Masking tape

White or colored cardstock for your cards

Paper plates

Acrylic paint (Green, red or gold are traditional.)

Glitter glue

Glitter

TOOLS

Pencil

Craft knife

Two mini paint rollers

INSTRUCTIONS

1 Spray the front of the foam letters with a good coat of adhesive. Also spray the piece of wood. Give the adhesive a few minutes to dry, and then stick the letters down on the wood—*face down and backwards*, as shown. You can leave the paper backing on the letters.

2 Now draw or print out some letters on a piece of copy paper. Trim the paper, leaving about a half inch around the letters, and tape it to the plastic. Then cut out your stencil letters. Remember to leave little connecting pieces for the center of the R. You're ready to print!

3 Cut and fold your cards. I cut 4 x 10-inch pieces of paper, and folded them to get 4 x 5-inch cards. Now put a dollop of paint on the paper plate. Roll out the paint with the roller, and roll a thin coat on your stamps.

4 Press your stamp down on the front of a card. Repeat until you print all your cards.

5 When they are dry, position your stencil over a card. Spread some glitter glue directly on a mini roller, and roll it over the stencil. Be sure to hold the stencil firmly to keep it from shifting around. Sprinkle some extra glitter on the glue if you want. Your cards are done—good job, buddy!

TEACHER AND PREACHER APPRECIATION PRESENTS

Christmas is a time of giving—to friends and family, of course, but also the mandatory "appreciation gifts" that one is expected to bestow upon your child's teachers and school bus drivers, your preacher, liquor store proprietor, mailman, trash guy, paperboy, and the like.

I was struck by a solution when I was helping my Auntie clean out her incredibly jumbled attic. From the smell I thought I was about to solve the mystery of my uncle's disappearance. But what I found was far, far worse—dozens of old Christmas sweaters, redolent with the rich funk of Christmas parties past. Anyone with any sense would have taken them out in the backyard with a rake and a can of gas, and burned them. But I saw potential there. There were a few cigarette burns and what I can only hope were—please God!—nog stains, but given that they were all 3XL, there were enough raw materials to make a decade's worth of "appreciation gifts"!

You could easily sew these beautiful cushions if you like, but I chose to use the bachelor's sewing machine—the hot glue gun. I'm going to use 2 slightly different methods for my pillows. Some I'll glue, and then add decorative yarn stitching around the edge, and for some I'll use rope or fringe trim.

MATERIALS

Christmas sweaters of various sizes

Yarn or embroidery floss

Yarn or beading needle

Trim lip cord tape, fringe trim tape, and/or ball trim tape in a Christmasy color

Polyester fiber fill (A 20-ounce bag should be enough for 3 pillows.)

Potpourri (optional)

TOOLS

Ruler

Marker

Scissors

Hot glue gun

INSTRUCTIONS

1 Lay your sweaters flat and determine the best area to cut out. I chose to make my pieces around 18 to 20 inches big. Try to position the design in the middle, and make sure to leave at least an extra inch on all four sides. Use the ruler and marker to mark your front square and cut out. Then lay that piece on the back of the sweater, and mark and cut your back square.

2 Now we are going to join the pieces. Line up the 2 pieces, one on top of the other, with the outside facing each other. For pillows with decorative yarn stitching around the edges, you just need to glue the edges of the fabric together. Use the glue gun to join a 1-inch-wide strip down 3 sides as shown.

3 For pillows with decorative trim tape edges, line up the edge of the trim tape with the edge of the good side of one piece of fabric. The fabric tape part of the trim should be next to the outside edge of the pillow fabric, as shown. Glue it all the way around, on all four sides. Then glue the other piece of fabric face down to that. Glue the second piece of fabric around 3 sides of the cushion, and only part of the fourth, leaving a gap of about 8 inches.

4 Now turn your pillow right side out and stuff it with polyester fill. You can even use the extra pieces of the sweater—as long as your glue seams hold, they'll never know. If you like, toss in a handful of potpourri. I made my own from peppermint after-dinner mints and pine sawdust.

 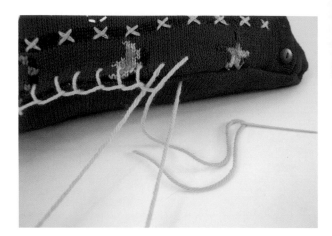

6 Glue the pillow completely closed. For a pillow
with a decorative stitch edging, stitch around
the outside with yarn or embroidery floss in
a blanket stitch as shown. Glue or stitch any
extra embellishments on the front—ric-rac,
bells, bows, tinsel—anything in your sewing
box that you want to get rid of.

7 You could wrap these in wrapping paper,
but I prefer to hand them to the recipient
unwrapped. It warms my heart to see the
gamut of fleeting emotions on their face
while they search for the words to thank me.

ABOUT THE AUTHOR

For many years Ross MacDonald has been a contributor to periodicals such as *Vanity Fair, The New York Times, The New Yorker, Newsweek, Time,* and *Rolling Stone,* creating illustrations and humor pieces. He also authored and illustrated four children's books. Yet all the while he led a secret double life designing and fabricating props for more than forty movies and television series, such as *Boardwalk Empire, The Knick,* David O Russel's movie *Kay's Baptism,* and Quentin Tarantino's *The Hateful Eight.* He has made everything from the book Bradley Cooper's character throws out the window in *Silver Linings Playbook,* to the titular Book of Secrets for the second *National Treasure* movie, baby's favorite book in *Baby's Day Out,* Nucky Thompson's checkbook and Arnold Rothstein's calling card for *Boardwalk Empire,* the morgue toe-tags in *The Knick,* the Pawnee town charter for *Parks and Recreation,* the Red Apple Tobacco tin in *The Hateful Eight,* and thousands of other props.

Born and raised in the backwoods of Canada—where crafting was not a luxury, it was a survival skill—he lived for many years in New York City before finally washing up on the bucolic shores of Connecticut.

ACKNOWLEDGMENTS

Special thanks to Holly McGhee for the idea and encouragement; to ace editor Jasmine Faustino at Flatiron; and to my wife, Lucy, and kids Jamie and Daisy, for all the help with crafts and photographs, and for putting up with a house crammed full of Christian kitsch.